THE BRINK

"In today's world we need not look very far for examples of leadership that fails us. Suddenly, a light shines in the dark and dares us to strive for something better. That light is Mark Hunter's powerful new book entitled *The Brink*. Using his own mountain-climbing experience as a well-lit path, the author lays bare his own triumphs and failures while breaking down that elusive edge that turns great leaders into influencers. Dare to travel farther without a guide? In your hands are the writings of a modern business sherpa. I suggest you mark it up. Test it. Dog-ear the pages and make it your own. You'll be glad you did."

—**Brad Szollose**, multigenerational management expert and
award-winning author, *Liquid Leadership: From Woodstock to Wikipedia*

"Mark Hunter has written an exhilarating book on leadership. He asks readers to journey deep inside themselves to discover the courage, will, and dedication that will allow them to face their limits and fears and become truly effective leaders."

—**Sean Brawley**, The Brawley Institute, and
the world's first certified inner game coach

"Mark Hunter's new book, *The Brink: How Great Leadership Is Invented*, is an excellent read, particularly for corporate leaders who feel in any way stuck. I particularly liked what he says about courage and risk and doing the impossible. Parts reminded me of Tracy Goss' book *The Last Word On Power*."

—**Timothy Askew**, CEO and founder,
Corporate Rain International

"As an adventurer, I resonated with the climbing stories and analogies in *The Brink*. However, the concepts and strategies are valid and powerful for anyone looking to improve as a leader in business and life. A great read!"

—**Heather Hansen O'Neill**, leadership and change speaker and
author, *Find Your Fire at Forty* and *Teams on Fire*

THE
BRINK

HOW GREAT LEADERSHIP
IS INVENTED

MARK HUNTER

New York

THE BRINK
HOW GREAT LEADERSHIP IS INVENTED

Published in New York, New York, by Morgan James Publishing. Morgan James and The Entrepreneurial Publisher are trademarks of Morgan James, LLC. www.MorganJamesPublishing.com

The Morgan James Speakers Group can bring authors to your live event. For more information or to book an event, visit The Morgan James Speakers Group at www.TheMorganJamesSpeakersGroup.com.

A **free** eBook edition is available
with the purchase of this print book.

CLEARLY PRINT YOUR NAME ABOVE IN UPPER CASE
Instructions to claim your free eBook edition:
1. Download the BitLit app for Android or iOS
2. Write your name in **UPPER CASE** on the line
3. Use the BitLit app to submit a photo
4. Download your eBook to any device

ISBN 978-1-63047-118-7 paperback
ISBN 978-1-63047-119-4 eBook
ISBN 978-1-63047-120-0 hardcover
Library of Congress Control Number:
2014934765

Cover Design by:
Chris Treccani
www.3dogdesign.net

Interior Design by:
Bonnie Bushman
bonnie@caboodlegraphics.com

In an effort to support local communities, increase awareness, and raise funds, Morgan James Publishing donates a percentage of all book sales for the life of each book to Habitat for Humanity Peninsula and Greater Williamsburg.

Get involved today. Visit
www.MorganJamesBuilds.com

Habitat
for Humanity®
Peninsula and
Greater Williamsburg
Building Partner

For Donna and Sherman Hunter,
my first leaders.

"The two most important days in your life are the
day you were born and the day you find out why."
—Mark Twain

TABLE OF CONTENTS

Acknowledgements   xv

Introduction   1

      The Brink   1

      Kilimanjaro   3

      The Brink Principle of Leadership   7

      The Big Eight Leadership Myths   8

      The Ten Principles of Generating Leadership   11
          on the Brink

      Chapter Snapshot   13

      Exercises/Questions   13

Chapter 1   Pick a Mountain   17

      Make It Big   17

      How to Pick Your Mountain   18

      Circumstances   19

      How a Leader Deals with Fear   20

      Vision and Mission   21

      New Problems—A Path to Leadership   23

      Gaps   24

      Chapter Snapshot   28

      Exercises/Questions   28

Chapter 2	Know the Answer to "What For?"	31
	Ask Early And Know the Answer	31
	The Brink Is Optional	32
	The Four Biggest Answers to the Question "What For?"	33
	Why > What > How	34
	Context	35
	Controlled Falls	38
	The Balance Myth	38
	Payoff	39
	Dying Before Going into Battle	41
	Reverence	41
	Parity	42
	Chapter Snapshot	44
	Exercises/Questions	45
Chapter 3	Choose Everything	47
	Crossroads	47
	Challenge Patterns	49
	Standing Ovations	50
	Not Choosing	51
	Unconditional Curiosity	51
	Pain	52
	Chapter Snapshot	54
	Exercises/Questions	54
Chapter 4	Practice	57
	What *Is* Practice?	57
	The Six Principles of Practice on the Brink	58
	Performance	59
	The Comfort Myth	60
	Stop Planning Picnics Based on the Weather	61

Clutch   62
The Disengagement Principle   62
Half Measures   63
Full Measures   64
Resilience   64
Forgiveness and Gratitude   65
Intentionality   66
Inspiration   67
Talent   67
Complacency   68
Open Heart   69
Chapter Snapshot   71
Exercises/Questions   72

Chapter 5   Collaborate   75
The Power of More Than One   75
Not All Leaders Need Followers   76
Three Components of Powerful Collaboration   76
Follow the Leader   77
Power   78
The Brink as Access to Power   79
Five Laws of Power on the Brink   79
The "Power Box" on the Brink   80
Power and the Open Heart   81
Power Leaks   82
The Other Truth   83
Common Power Leaks   83
None of Us Is as Great as All of Us   84
Fundamentals of a Winning Team   85
Leadership Corollaries   86
Commodities and Assets   87
Chapter Snapshot   89
Exercises/Questions   90

Chapter 6	Take Ownership	93
	Over Here	93
	Ownership Is Leadership	94
	The One	94
	Ferocity	95
	Causation	96
	Innovation	96
	Influence	97
	Intentionality	97
	Urgency vs. Emergency	98
	The Urgency/Emergency Matrix	98
	"The Fierce Urgency of Now"	100
	Drama	101
	The Status Quo	101
	Chapter Snapshot	103
	Exercises/Questions	104
Chapter 7	Trust	107
	Trust as Faith	107
	Possibility vs. Probability	107
	Trust in Practice	108
	Burn Your Boats	109
	Hope	109
	The "How Trap"	110
	Expectation	110
	Risk	111
	Risk Loading	111
	Generating Trust	112
	Chapter Snapshot	114
	Exercises/Questions	114
Chapter 8	Welcome Fear and Adversity	117
	Fear, Revisited	117
	Normalizing Obstacles	118

The End of Normal		119
Visibility		119
Transparency		120
Deviance		121
Walking Tiger Safaris		121
Adversity		123
The Great Fail		124
Suffering Is Optional		124
Closets		125
Sabotage		126
Success Is Optional		127
Drama, Revisited		127
The Path of Less Convenience		128
The Conflicting Commitment Model		129
Unreasonable		130
The Evidence Myth		130
Excuse Proof		131
The Persistence Principle		132
Being Willing Without Wanting To		133
Problems		133
The Leadership Matrix		134
Stories		135
Chapter Snapshot		137
Exercises/Questions		139
Chapter 9	Create Integrity	143
	Integrity Redefined	143
	Should	144
	Closet Inauthenticity	145
	Reintegration	146
	Clarity/Peace	148
	The Motivation Myth	148
	Commitment	149
	Relentlessness	150

	Shortcuts	151
	Bold Declarations	151
	Safety	152
	Chapter Snapshot	153
	Exercises/Questions	153
Chapter 10	Be Unstoppable	157
	Stop First	157
	Choose It	157
	"Possibility Interruptus"	158
	Resilience and Results	158
	The Art of Relentless Pursuit	159
	Hard Work	159
	Runner's High	160
	Surrender	161
	Courage	162
	Desire	162
	Two Conversations	163
	The Insight Trap	164
	Chapter Snapshot	166
	Exercises/Questions	167
Summary		169
	The Big Picture	169
	Who	170
	No	170
	Inevitability	171
	Squirrels	171
	Scope	173
	An Impassioned Request	173
About the Author		175

"Reasonable people adapt themselves to the world. Unreasonable people attempt to adapt the world to themselves. All progress, therefore, depends on unreasonable people."

—George Bernard Shaw

ACKNOWLEDGEMENTS

As with any great endeavor, contributions from countless individuals helped create this book through content, support, and inspiration. This section does not do justice to those who have had a hand in making this book possible. Thank you to all of you who have been a part of *The Brink*'s genesis and completion. Whether you see your name here or not, your contribution has not gone unnoticed!

First, thank you, Mom, for being the first leader who made me want to be a leader. Thank you for the mountains you chose to climb and for the love and respect you gave and taught Todd and me. Without you, none of this would have been possible—and not just for the obvious reason of your giving me life itself. You also gave birth to the insatiable desire in me to lead and make a difference in the world for those who cannot always see that others can make a difference for them. They and I owe you our eternal gratitude. I love you more than ever, and I honor you with this book. While it still hurts every single day not to be able to hold you and see your smile, you are always with me.

Thank you, Dad, for everything—especially for your love and trust and friendship. You are still the man I aspire to be when I grow up. Who I am in the world is a direct reflection of you and all that you have taught me. You have been the foundation and the model for so much of what made this possible. Who you and Pat are in your own lives is both inspiring and heartwarming. Thank you for loving each other and for loving me so much through everything that we have gone through. And Pat, thank you for your love and friendship and for the work you have done in conflict resolution across the globe that helps me see what is possible.

Todd, thank you for always leading in your own way. You are an inspiration to me every day. Lucas and Logan are lucky to have you as a father, and I am lucky to have you as my brother and friend. Thank you for making Mom a grandmother and for making us all proud to have you in our lives. I love you and am always behind you, up or down, close or far.

Thank you to my wife and best friend, Christa. Absolutely every word that is written here is a reflection of who you have been for me over countless weeks, months, and years of work, travel, and focus on this effort. You are a gift, and the one who inspired, challenged, and stood with me where no one else saw to inspire, challenge, or stand. Thank you for seeing all the messy corners and edges of me and of this work and still relating to us both as whole and complete. I love you with all that I am. You are my favorite story to tell and the source of my ability to make a difference with so many people in the world.

Thank you to all my clients over the past 19 years who have given me the forum to explore these ideas and practices in my endeavor to make a difference for each of you. All of you are represented in this work and in my gratitude.

Thank you to Accomplishment Coaching for giving me the platform to train other coaches and be trained in such a rigorous and compassionate environment. Specifically, thank you, Christopher McAuliffe, for your vision, commitment, and friendship. Thank you, Jodi Larson, for your grace, heart, and constant brilliance. Thank you, Samadi Demme, for your love and partnership that always come from the heart. Thank you, Marita Bolles, for your strength and inspiration in the face of all that stopped me for so long. When I couldn't see a way out, you showed me over and over again that there was one, while always reminding me that I didn't need one. Thank you to all the leaders and leaders in training who have trusted me to train them and to be trained by them in the process. You are all gifts, and there are parts of you in every page that follows.

Thank you, Jeffrey Jabon and Antoine Joseph, for always being my best friends in the worst of times. Your patience, trust, and loyalty are the glue that held this vision together and were the source of many of the stories told in these pages (and many more that were left out).

Thank you, Kathy Metcalf, for walking with me through the darkest of places while always being the light and trusting me to come out the other side. Thank you for always challenging me to lead the way myself. Without your courage to stand in that horror with me, none of this would have been possible. Every person I make a difference for is touched in part by the difference you have made for me. Thank you for seeing me before I could see myself and for introducing me to what have become the favorite parts of my life. I love you always for all of it.

Thank you, Morgan James Publishing, for your vision and for being inspired by what lies in these pages enough to invest in both me and this work.

A special thanks to Katherine Metres for partnering with me in the editing and completion of this book. Thank you for your unwavering integrity, expertise, and professionalism. You are the example of an artist and a collaborator as an editor and a change agent. Thank you for both challenging me and trusting me every step of the way. You had the courage to say what was so at every turn, while maintaining the course we were on and honoring every part of our partnership, both in spirit and in fact. Your gift is the brilliance with which you chipped away at the pieces to reveal the gold in these pages.

Thank you, all!

"Opportunity is missed by many people because it is dressed in overalls and looks like work."

—Mark Twain

INTRODUCTION

THE BRINK

Leadership is not promised, born, or inherited. It is chosen, practiced, and created. This book is for those interested in taking on that choice, practice, and creation.

Becoming a leader is not easy. It's not comfortable or intuitive, either. As a result, real, effective leadership is scarce. Leadership requires a level of commitment and resilience that most are unwilling to practice. Many people call themselves leaders, but few live up to the title. They're not bad people; they simply aren't leaders.

This book is inspired by a global gap that I am committed to closing. Today's world is suffering from a gap in leadership. Almost every major problem in the world (financial crises, crime, violence, global warming, etc.) can be fundamentally linked to a gap in leadership. In most cases, that gap is not even clearly identified, let alone addressed to any sufficient degree.

The tragedy, though, lies beyond the fact that the leadership gap has not been identified or addressed. The real tragedy is that on some level we all *know* there is a grave lack of leadership in our societies, yet few do anything about it. There are people with the desire to see change occur, but most of them behave as if it's someone else's job … and he or she should be arriving at any moment to make things better.

Well, here's the wake-up call: That someone is you. The only effective way to respond to this global leadership gap is to step into it.

The big question is … Will you?

"The brink" is a leadership development methodology that is based on a simple fundamental philosophy: our leadership is developed on the brink of our most difficult challenges. When challenged, we are required to rise to the occasion, and as a result, we grow. The process is similar to muscular development: our muscles grow stronger as a result of repairs that take place to knit back together small tears caused by exertion. The process for developing leadership is built into our lives from the time we are children. It's an inherent gift made available by our DNA programming, but if left unpracticed for very long, leadership skills will atrophy like any unused muscle.

Unfortunately, many would-be leaders have become addicts of comfort, safety, and security instead of the challenges that would grow their leadership. Most have become slaves to the changing weather patterns of whether they "feel like it" or not in each moment—or whether goals seem "reasonable." They have lost sight of the power that exists in facing challenges.

Why have would-be leaders become so complacent? Mostly because they believe that they simply don't "have to" lead anymore at the level I suggest here. In the age of the Internet, quick money, the cell phone, and fear (of tough economic times, terrorism, the future, etc.), we live a remote-control life, the goals of which are to eradicate risk and to experience as much ease and comfort as possible. The impulse to stick to a challenging commitment even when we don't feel like it anymore has been lost to an entire market of exit strategies and avoidance techniques. Over time, our instinct to press on and remain committed to our goals, even when accomplishing them is hardest, have succumbed to the seduction of what's easy.

I call the type of leadership that has replaced the real thing "armchair leadership." Armchair leaders must first feel comfortable and safe before choosing to lead. Such "leaders" provide little satisfaction in a world starving for true leadership. Given the specific challenges we face in the world today, the culture of comfort addiction in leadership is simply no longer effective or tolerable.

It's time for *you* to step into leadership. A vast majority of this book is committed to the idea that we don't need one great leader to lead us all, but rather we need to choose to develop the leader in each of us. This is not an easy solution; after all, it requires individual responsibility and a commitment to generating solutions to the very problems for which we have become so adept at blaming others.

The word "invented" appears in the title of this book on purpose. Its use asserts that leadership literally can be (and needs to be) created from scratch in each moment, by each of us, in order to meet the challenge that is currently at hand. Leadership is not a generic solution to anything or something that exists separate from the individual wielding it. Instead, it is a way of being and a practice that one chooses to take on and generate from within.

I write this book because I have used the process I will describe in the pages that follow to develop leaders for well over a decade, and it works. It works if you are willing to step to the brink and start climbing.

KILIMANJARO

In 1999, while climbing Mount Kilimanjaro in Tanzania, I came across parts of myself that I had buried and hidden away for the first 29 years of my life—parts that I had been scared to confront but that the side of that mountain demanded I face and conquer. Those parts included fear, discomfort, self-loathing, success, anger, pain, and my tolerance for each.

At 19,341 feet, Kilimanjaro's one of the few 18,000+ foot peaks in the world that is accessible without supplemental oxygen and technical gear (for some routes). The route I took is called the Marangu Route (called the

"Coca-Cola Route" by the locals because of its popularity and accessibility). I declined the option of supplemental oxygen, since the gradual ascent along that route allows climbers' bodies time to acclimate to the altitude as they climb.

This gradual ascent creates an interesting effect on the climber: the cruel illusion of multiple peaks. Along the five-day ascent, I glanced up hundreds of times and said to myself, "That *has* to be the top." But each time, it was not.

You get there, or to a ridge line near to it, and realize that you are not only not close but you also don't seem any closer. In addition, for the second half of the climb, you can see the peak itself, and it appears deceptively close. The mental challenge is that it is actually so far away that you never appear to make any progress toward it.

The final stage of the climb begins at Kibo Hut, a camp located at 15,520 feet, just below the scree line. (Scree is volcanic ash, which appears like black baby powder piled a foot deep in every direction around you. The scree line is the line above which the mountainside is covered in scree.) At that altitude, your breathing is labored due to the lack of oxygen, it's bitter cold, and you're exposed to high winds on the side of a treeless moonscape at aircraft cruising altitude. Edema (fluid in your lungs and brain) is a possible lethal effect of spending too much time and exertion at that altitude, and yet, you're about to take a lot of time and make a lot of exertion there.

At this base camp, your job is to somehow sleep upon arrival in the mid-afternoon after climbing for over four days already to get there, through your shortness of breath, exhaustion, and pain. The idea is to wake up at 2 a.m. the next day and climb 4,000 feet to the summit before the sun rises. Then this part you will never forget: you spend eight hours climbing at a 30-degree angle in shin-deep scree. For every three steps you take, you slide back one. As you also contend with sleep deprivation, exhaustion, lack of oxygen, high winds, and bitter cold, this backsliding is emotionally devastating.

Your mind screams at you to turn around. Your body demands that you do so and shuts down occasionally by making you dizzy and clumsy, with bouts of dry heaving. Your circumstances and the environment are completely unreasonable and irrational relative to what you are familiar to.

And that's exactly why you keep going. Each footstep and subsequent "footslide" become deliberate acts of defiance fueled by curiosity about the unknown. You throw everything you've got at this mountain over and over, and it seems to never end—but somehow you *know* it has to.

You think to yourself, *I know there is a "top" to this thing, and if I can just put one foot in front of the other a few more times, maybe I'll find it. And if I don't find it after those few steps, I'm gonna take a few more.* There's a simplicity to it that's both maddening and comforting at the same time. Your emotions and mental state run the full range. There are rage, elation, tears, and joy at seeing the grandeur of the earth with the naked eye. Then you feel mild insanity alternating with courage, resolve, and terror, followed by calm surrender at the certainty that you will die there. Ultimately you experience a powerful and paradoxical mixture of pain, resilience, resignation, power, and a sense of presence when you realize you are still alive. Close to the peak of Kilimanjaro, I felt this sensation so poignantly and distinctly that I have drawn on it regularly over the 13 years since then in times of adversity and challenges that I could not see the other side of.

That type of challenge teaches you a great deal about yourself, and it changes you. The truth is, you've either experienced that part of yourself, or you have stayed in your comfort zone and avoided it. In the thick of a painful challenge that requires all you can give, you either move forward through it, or it eats you up and breaks you. Either way, you discover something deeply intimate and primal in those moments; you learn that that experience has a unique value that can only be accessed through the immense challenge of it.

I spent seven days climbing that mountain: five days up, two days down. I only spent 90 seconds at the top, but 90 seconds was more than enough. It turns out that the brutal physical conditions, the incredible views, and the height of the peak didn't ultimately matter. What stays with me today, rather, is having discovered exactly what it took to get there. The real ascent took place inside myself while climbing Kilimanjaro, and it changed me forever.

The poet Kahlil Gibran wrote, "Out of suffering have emerged the strongest souls; the most massive characters are seared with scars." What I discovered in the very dark places I visited on the side of that mountain were the depths of both my despair and joy, the breadth of my being, and the resolve within to do the impossible—discoveries far more important than any view.

Not all mountains are measured in feet or meters. Some mountains are measured in adversity, possibility (or impossibility), fear, a self-selected challenge, a promise, pain, a declared goal, joy, the depth of the unknown, or the scope of one's vision. Both before and after Kilimanjaro, I have faced many mountains along my path. Some I intentionally created for myself, while others were thrust upon me. But all of them changed and shaped me into the leader I would eventually become.

In truth, there have been such mountains at every turn of my life: the violence I saw growing up in Brooklyn in the 1970s and 80s; the sudden death of my mother when I was 20; the Wilderness First Responder Training I took in 1997 and used at Ground Zero in 2001; becoming a certified rescue diver; the multiple companies I have started, sold, or lost; Cross Fit; trying out at Development Camp for the 1993 U.S. National Lightweight Rowing team; and taking on the coach and leadership training programs I have completed and currently lead. All have been gifts in their own way, though inexplicably painful and seemingly impossible at times. It is this act of facing internal challenges out in the external world that creates true leaders. This is what the brink is about.

Leadership is a term thrown around in the world today in a very cavalier way, but I'm certain that it means something much different for those of us who have suffered the gift of climbing a mountain of our own to get there.

Play this game with me right now: list the three biggest accomplishments you have created in your life. Write them down on a piece of paper and take a good long look at them. Be present with them again, with the process you went through, the struggles, the challenges, the elation, and the sense of accomplishment. Now ask yourself: At the beginning, did each of these endeavors strike you as easy, comfortable, or safe? Next ask yourself: Was your struggle worth it?

I'm guessing that your answers were "No" and "Yes," in that order. Now ask yourself: Are you willing to give up on your next great accomplishment to avoid being challenged, getting uncomfortable, or feeling unsafe? If your answer is "No," you are already on your way toward creating purposeful leadership in your life and in the world. We will take the next steps together in these pages.

Now, think of the highest height you believe you can climb—the point to which you believe you can succeed or grow. Moving through that point, not around it, will be the key to your success as a leader. In his book *The Big Leap*, Gay Hendricks calls the point at which we perceive we cannot stretch any further an "upper limit problem," but I call it a habit. Too many people have developed the habit of, in effect, only placing bets on races they know they can win—but this only impedes their path to greatness.

Mountains are picturesque and enticing to look at from afar, and like most large endeavors, become more imposing as you approach. They can become terrifying as you start to climb. It is through facing those fears and continuing to climb that you develop yourself and your capacity for leadership.

If you are willing to make the climb despite the uncertainty, this book will serve as a guide to encourage you and help you overcome the obstacles to reaching the summit.

THE BRINK PRINCIPLE OF LEADERSHIP
Definition
    brink [brɪnk]
    n
    1.   the edge, border, or verge of a steep place—*the brink of the precipice*
    2.   the highest point; top—*the sun fell below the brink of the hill*
    3.   boundary - the greatest possible degree of something
    4.   the limit beyond which something happens or changes; a crucial or critical point, especially of a situation or state beyond which success or catastrophe occurs—*the brink of war; the brink of disaster*

Typically we think of being on the brink of something as a dangerous place we're about to "fall" off of, or an edge we are about to slip down. Unfortunately, that's also the way many people relate to leadership. This attitude is defined by their attachment to power, title, status, influence, popularity, or emotional reaction to events. Let's take a moment to address the eight most prominent leadership myths you will likely encounter.

THE BIG EIGHT LEADERSHIP MYTHS

Myth #1: Leadership is either born in people or not.

Of the many myths about leadership, this one is the most rampant and damaging. Consider that the greatest lie told about leadership is that someone was born/gifted with it and it's for him or her to lead, not for you. Ironically, this one was created in order to keep some people from taking on leadership, by preserving it for a few "chosen ones." But take heart: leadership is for anyone who is committed to it, anyone willing to do what it takes to create and embody it.

Myth #2: Leadership requires force or leverage over others.

This myth is a relic of the old paradigm of leadership that called for leaders to assert themselves as such by creating hierarchy and influence over others. These leaders needed to do this, because—fearful of losing their influence or perceived power over others—they fundamentally believed that fear was the best tool to leverage results. Power and leadership do go hand in hand, but power in this model comes *from* leadership, not *to* leaders. Power on the brink is only relevant in the *service* of leading.

Myth #3: Everyone loves a leader.

Winston Churchill said, "You have enemies? Good. That means you've stood for something in your life." And he was right. If you stand powerfully as a leader for something, enemies will sprout like weeds.

Leadership creates opposition and has consequences. Leaders will create differences in opinion and position wherever they go. And that's not a bad thing. Not only will some people not love you, but some will hate and work against you. Leaders need to expect this and consider it normal.

Even those you lead will not always love you—and that's okay. The truth is that leaders don't need to be loved by those they lead. Leaders are much better off seeking love from people other than those they lead. It's important to note that the need to be loved by everyone will actually get in the way of leading, because it will ultimately become more important to the leader than the goal itself.

Myth #4: Leaders are not afraid.

On the contrary, leaders are smart enough to be very afraid. Leaders are often tasked with taking on challenges that are inherently scary. In fact, leaders are drawn to these types of challenges. They are also courageous enough that fear does not stop them from leading but actually causes them to step up their game. Leaders are masters at playing in the presence of and working through their fear. They learn to operate with fear as part of their process—to actually leverage that fear into action and movement, allowing for better navigation through problems that arise along the way.

Myth #5: People will automatically follow a leader.

There is nothing automatic about causing people to follow you. Finding followers might initially be easy, but leaders must do the work to entice others to follow their vision and then continue to keep them committed. This process is referred to as "enrollment." Savvy leaders know how crucial it is to continually re-inspire those they lead with their vision and mission, in order to sustain momentum and maintain results.

Myth #6: Leaders are experts who know all the answers.

Not only is this not true, but true leaders are fully aware that they don't and won't know all the answers. Leaders are prepared to encounter places where they will get stuck and do not know the answers. The key is that they also see themselves as capable of finding the answers when they need to.

The truth is that expert knowledge and past experience have almost *no bearing* on future success. Leaders know this and focus instead on the success of the team and the mission at hand over their "expertise." Oftentimes ego will cause a leader to become overly focused on "knowing all the answers," but the most effective and impactful leaders focus instead on the intended result they are after and doing what it takes to get there. They focus on the expertise they need rather than needing to be seen as experts by others. Leaders are experts in leading but usually not expert in every aspect of the endeavor they undertake as a leader.

Myth #7: Leaders are always positive.
No. (And I just modeled it here.) Savvy leaders will intentionally deliver messages in the tone and context that will have the most impact, and sometimes that means using the negative. We see sports coaches and leaders in movies getting tough on their teams and unloading on them in order to intentionally drive up the fight in them to turn a losing situation around. Leadership requires the ability to recognize and adapt the method of delivery and context in which the message is delivered to the situation or character of the person to be influenced. Sometimes a swift kick in the pants is what's needed, and while the outcome may be positive, the delivery isn't always positive or "pleasant."

Myth #8: Leaders require followers.
In the past, leadership was mostly defined as the ability to inspire people to follow. It was measured by the number of followers we could accrue and how far we could get them to move in a certain direction. It was ego based and limited in both scope and depth, having little to do with any clear vision or mission.

Today's leader is faced with the challenge and reality of universal access to information and resources. Millions of Twitter followers can be collected via one television appearance or other media notoriety. Because of the sheer ease of accessing followers, leadership today is required on a more grassroots level than at almost any time since industrialization. It's actually required on such a grassroots level that it needs to start internally. We each need to start to relate to ourselves as leaders in our lives, endeavors, relationships, and anywhere else we find ourselves, first. Only then can we effectively lead others.

What that requires is a level of responsibility for the world around us that does not require instruction or inspiration from others and that does not necessarily feed the ego. We call this "taking ownership" of what happens. Taking ownership is the new leadership dynamic, and it's what the brink is all about.

The old leadership paradigm required force, fearlessness, followers, and the right leadership pedigree. In that model, you might notice that most of the energy is focused externally, at managing the world around oneself, along with public opinion. Managing then becomes the job, but there are so many different external factors to control that the job is a futile one.

The brink is not for that leader. In the new leadership paradigm, the leader approaches the brink with an inward focus. The brink serves to create an opportunity to rise not just to the occasion when needed but also to a new "floor"—both for leaders and the teams we lead. In other words, the same way we habitually create ceilings for possibility and upward movement, we can also intentionally create floors below which we are no longer willing to operate. *We can even make our old ceilings our new floors.*

From that new floor, the brink allows you a foundation to play bigger than you thought possible. That's because you are no longer engaging in the distracting games that are comfortable and familiar to you and that have you playing small. There is no risk of slipping and falling into leadership. There is only the risk of creating such huge shifts in your own experience as a leader—playing big—that you cause a ripple effect around you.

Let's get started.

THE TEN PRINCIPLES OF GENERATING LEADERSHIP ON THE BRINK

In my work as a coach in various capacities over the past 19 years, I've discovered 10 distinct principles that contribute to the generation and growth of leadership:

1. **Pick a mountain**
2. **Know the answer to "What for?"**

3. Choose everything
4. Practice
5. Collaborate
6. Take ownership
7. Trust
8. Welcome fear and adversity
9. Create integrity
10. Be unstoppable

The remainder of this book will explore each of these principles in great detail. I don't pretend that these 10 principles constitute "the right way," but I've coached leaders, developed my own leadership, regularly created unusually large results, and led teams very successfully over a long period of time using them. The invitation is for you to integrate these principles into your own leadership, put in the pieces that fit, and leave out what doesn't. To be clear, a necessary component of leadership development is a willingness not only to welcome but also to seek out a certain degree of discomfort. Be aware of the difference between a lack of progress and simply being unwilling to be patient and uncomfortable along the way.

INTRODUCTION

CHAPTER SNAPSHOT

- The brink's core philosophy: the process of facing some great challenge will create the leader within you.
- The solution to the leadership challenges/gaps that the world faces today starts with your individual leadership and commitment to closing those gaps.
- The new leadership paradigm—the brink—requires an inward focus rather than external management.

The Eight Leadership Myths

1. Leadership is either born in people or not.
2. Leadership requires force/leverage over others.
3. Everyone loves a leader.
4. Leaders are not afraid.
5. People will automatically follow a leader.
6. Leaders are experts who know all the answers.
7. Leaders are always positive.
8. Leaders require followers.

- The brink is an invitation—you can choose to accept it or not.
- The brink is a challenge—you can choose to take it on or not.
- The brink requires willingness to bear or even intentionally pursue discomfort.

EXERCISES/QUESTIONS

1. Leadership Emulation List—Make a list of five leaders you would like to emulate and write why.
2. Notice leaders around you practicing leadership on the old paradigm (i.e., inside of the leadership myths listed above).
3. Notice your expectations that you or others who wish to be leaders should fulfill the eight myths identified here.

4. What goals have you only dreamed about that would make it worth it for you to put yourself up to something bigger than you see possible? Make a list and hang it where you will see it every day.

"The ultimate measure of a man is not where he stands in moments of comfort and convenience but where he stands at times of challenge and controversy."
—Martin Luther King, Jr.

CHAPTER 1

PICK A MOUNTAIN

MAKE IT BIG

As I mentioned in the Introduction, not all mountains are measured in feet or meters. For the purposes of leadership, the metaphor of a mountain as an endeavor is useful in that it describes something big with which to challenge ourselves—typically something big enough that we cannot readily see all the components of it at the outset. This makes us test the edges of what we think is possible. These edges are where change and leadership happen, and where new possibilities live.

Most of the time, we live in the realm of experience that includes what we relate to as reasonable, and this habit has us playing in the same old comfortable sandbox over and over. The mountain you want to pick in the brink model is the unreasonable, uncomfortable one: Run a marathon over a 5K. Stay when it feels better to leave. Take the CrossFit class instead of the treadmill. Ask the hottest girl in the bar for her number rather than sitting with your friends for the rest of the night. Write the book rather than reading someone else's. Choose the stairs each day rather than the escalator. Move through your despair rather than avoiding it. Own your illness instead of being victimized by it. Pick something bigger than you have before, and do it on purpose—with a purpose in mind.

The brink rests firmly on the notion that leadership can be created by intentionally putting an individual or team up to something quite challenging, thus encouraging the growth and development of the individuals and the team to have the qualities and tools needed to climb to the top. To be clear, this requires something specific from the leader and each team member: intentionality.

HOW TO PICK YOUR MOUNTAIN

Chris Warner, author of *High Altitude Leadership* and CEO of Earth Treks, has led expeditions to the peaks of Mt. Everest and K2, the highest and second-highest mountains on earth. He's famous for saying, "Don't reach the peak and miss the point." Everest lost its magic for Warner once hundreds of people per day were able to pay to be dragged to the top. It no longer held the magic, the challenge, and the draw of the unknown for him. So he went after K2 specifically because it was the path less taken.

I've heard Warner speak about his experiences with life and death on the sides of the most dangerous mountains on earth, and I came away crystal clear about a few things: First, he sought the mountains he chose specifically for their degree of mystery and uncharted routes, *because* they were less known. Second, talking about the mountain from the comfort of a chair means very little. It's the very experience of doubt, impossibility, discomfort, and struggle with the mountain itself that creates the space for leadership to develop and expand. Finally, he discovered a tipping point in his personal development when he began to choose this greater path of discomfort, leadership, and pioneering discovery in all aspects of life. *He sought it out.* From that foundational choice point, he became committed to it on such a fundamental level that it actually drove what he was looking for and ultimately what he would find.

Pick your mountain on purpose. Choose your mountain in service of the leadership that you are committed to in the first place. It should reflect your intention, purpose, and leadership goals, in service of the team if there is one. Without the mountain, leadership has little footing on which to stand its ground. The brink requires an endeavor that creates or can express the leader's calling, and the size of the endeavor tends to dictate the size of the calling.

From there, the process of leadership development becomes about setting yourself and/or your team up to live into the greatness on which the target is set. That's the fundamental mechanism that makes leadership accessible: creating a big game to live into, or in this case, *lead* into. Too often leadership is conjured in a vacuum with the same old familiar challenges, circumstances, and contexts that have existed all along. Attempting to lead from inside our comfort zone has gotten us here—to the results we have already produced—but will not get us to the next level. In fact, it has us far more focused on creating comfort than on leadership, vision, or mission.

CIRCUMSTANCES

Einstein said, "You cannot create the solution to a problem from the same set of circumstances that created it in the first place." This suggests that one change the "circumstances." In the brink model, however, circumstances are like weather; they are constantly changing and will not stop or go away. Your job as a leader is to normalize this and produce the result in the face of it, the same way you go to work whether it's raining out or sunny. The key to this part of the brink is your choosing leadership in the face of circumstances, rather than relying on the circumstances to change first.

The gift in the mountain and the circumstances that will arise from here is that you get to raise the stakes, increase the gradient, and up the challenge as you see appropriate. This challenge will cause you and your team to step into new, uncharted territory and call forth your innate response to adversity. So stop trying to change your circumstances and get to leading in the face of them instead.

Bet you didn't think we'd start off by challenging Einstein, did you? But that's exactly what leadership takes. Nothing is sacred. To lead as you've only dreamed of leading, you must play bigger than you ever have before.

Gay Hendricks, who wrote about the upper limit problem, talks about finding a "beacon." Once identified, a beacon can be used to guide us toward our mountain and help us override our upper limit problem. It enables us to stop the upper limit from outlining precisely how good we think we can have it and how big we think we can make our wins and successes. An example of a beacon is a mission or vision that is big enough and important enough to us to call us forth again and again through adversity and setbacks. It's something bigger than ourselves that we are so invested in creating that we will generate resilience as needed in service of it, and do what it takes to overcome obstacles in our path.

We can use our awareness of the beacon to put ourselves on the brink intentionally, with a clear vision of what is at the summit of our mountain. The beacon can also help us generate awareness and come to terms with the moment that will occur at some point along the climb when we inevitably encounter our upper limit. That awareness gives us the ability not to be stopped by it but instead recognize it as we approach it and prepare to climb through it.

On the brink, you get to throw yourself against and into something worthy of both your greatness and your fear. From there you not only get to see the view from the top, but you also get to see the parts of you that are newly discovered and unleashed along the way. You get to uncover the possibilities you have buried, give permission to the places to which you have not allowed access, forgive the unforgivable, and play on the border of the impossible. The time to stop waiting to get started is fully yours to decide. Your leadership and the things you choose to put yourself up to—or not—are inextricably linked to making this clear and powerful decision.

HOW A LEADER DEALS WITH FEAR

Idrisa, my Tanzanian climbing guide on the mountain, taught me powerful lessons about leadership and the role of fear. I was a 29-year-old wearing tech gear, climbing boots, and five layers of synthetic moisture-wicking clothes. He was a 19-year-old wearing a long-sleeved cotton shirt and a light jacket to go with his sneakers. As we climbed through my nausea, pain, exhaustion, and distraction, he stayed focused, coaching me along the way to take one step at a time and stop looking at the top. He always smiled (which was at times maddening and at other times the only thing keeping me upright) through all the challenges we faced along the way. He even helped carry some of my gear at some points. (I had chosen to skip hiring a porter as well, so I was carrying 50 pounds of my own gear.)

Idrisa was poised and courageous in the face of the weather we encountered and the unconscious climber suffering from lethal high altitude sickness whom we saw being rushed down the mountain in a wheelbarrow by his guides in an attempt to save his life. We never learned whether that climber lived or died.

Idrisa tackled countless other challenges on the side of that mountain with grace— including being responsible for both our survival and success. I asked him if he was afraid at one point, and he said to me, "Yes. It is not smart to be on this mountain and not be afraid. It deserves our fear. Fear is why we climb it. Fear is also what makes it possible to climb it and stay alive at the same time."

This contrasts with Franklin D. Roosevelt's famously saying, "The only thing we have to fear is fear itself." Fear is not something to be avoided; fear is a necessary ally if we let it inform us to take right action instead of letting it goad us into taking no action.

Courage is action taken in the presence of fear, not in the absence of it. Leaders know this and move forward with their fear present rather than trying to eliminate it. Idrisa was a leader at 19 years old, wearing sneakers at 19,000 ft. He had no formal leadership training, just a mission, a vision, and a serious mountain to climb. Leaders don't always *look* like leaders, but on the sides of the mountains they climb, they are unmistakable.

VISION AND MISSION

The most successful leaders on the brink have a vision that is clear and a mission they are undertaking decisively in service of that vision. An effective vision is at the same time concise, contextually expansive, and immediately enticing to the team and to others considering joining the team. What I mean by "contextually expansive" is that it expands the filter through which we see both the mountain we have chosen and the possibility of successfully climbing it. The vision is the glue that holds a team together through all challenging circumstances that will arise. The vision supplies the answer to the question, "Why are we climbing this mountain?"

For example, all the members of the team at NASA that first put a man on the moon were crystal clear that the answer to that question for them was "Get a man landed on the moon and then back home safely, by the end of the decade." That clarity of vision and answer to the question "What for?" carried them through delays, setbacks, failures, the challenges of Projects Mercury and Gemini, and ultimately to Project Apollo. Apollo 11 successfully completed the mission on July 20, 1969.

The mission needs to be impactful and specific; it describes the endeavor that the team works toward. The mission is our proverbial mountain in the brink model and answers the question, "What are we doing in service of our vision?" It needs to be both reflective of the vision and inspiring to its participants. The mission must align with the principles and intentions of the team, and include everyone involved.

The other vital characteristic of a successful mission is that there must be full subscription across the board. Both the mission and the team can suffer dire consequences if the team lacks full commitment. In climbing real mountains, that consequence can be death. In business and other goals, lack of commitment can mean problems that put the team and future of the organization in jeopardy.

Balancing vision with mission is often tricky for leaders and can become a quagmire if not handled deftly. The brink model requires that leaders clearly outline the vision and mission for both themselves and the team before taking on the mission and climbing the mountain. Here, leaders also take responsibility for engaging themselves and the team in how the vision and mission serve them personally. In addition, leaders must maintain their commitment through the storms, setbacks, disagreements, and lulls in action that will inevitably occur. Leadership requires a deep understanding that enrollment in a mission and vision is an ongoing process, like nurturing a seed that has been planted. Teams need to know that their leaders remain enrolled in the mission and vision regardless of the circumstances with which they are faced.

Leaders on the brink are aware that people do not initially follow a vision or a mission; they follow a leader *into* that vision and mission. Leaders on the brink need to fully understand that *they* are the direct connection between those they lead and the vision that they hold. Leaders provide the initial road map to the opportunity of the brink. The vision simply gives platform to leadership and direction to the leaders' velocity. Since they are the force that people follow at first, leaders must be willing to consistently present themselves as such.

A vision is simply an idea that is big and projected into the tangible future. One can argue that an idea doesn't even *exist* until and unless a leader chooses to own and champion it. The vision a leader embodies will be the reason the community or team becomes committed in the first place— it's the rallying point for the energy of the members.

NEW PROBLEMS—A PATH TO LEADERSHIP

Leaders on the brink generate new problems. They stretch into new areas and risk the unknown; this inevitably presents them with new obstacles or circumstances they have not seen before. But this process of generating and overcoming new problems creates growth. We only grow when we step out of the familiar and play in new unknown areas. Being outside our comfort zone creates new experiences and challenges, and forces us to adapt in order to thrive. This is also a fundamental part of the brink. In our NASA example of putting a man on the moon and bringing him back safely within the decade, that new problem they faced actually created the new discoveries and possibilities that ultimately made it happen. The unfamiliarity of the challenge itself generated the required creativity and ingenuity to meet it.

Isn't the world full of enough problems without creating new ones? Well, on the brink, the problems a leader creates are not really "problems," in the same way that the extra mile you add to your run isn't a problem. It's a stretch, a place to sharpen our edge, an opportunity. Leaders look for these places. They revel in new problems. They do this by becoming experts at both looking for and identifying gaps. This is precisely what the engineers and designers at NASA did that had them be successful in the face of their new problem.

GAPS

A gap is simply the space between where we are today and where we want to be. This is often the space that most people identify as their problem. As a coach, I regularly work with very successful people and teams who create powerful declarations and big goals, and then instantly begin to describe what a problem it is that they have not yet met those goals!

It's both interesting and important to note that this is a fundamental reason for many of the issues in leadership we deal with today both in the business and social spheres. The basic belief that where we are is *wrong* simply because we have goals for something greater that we have not yet achieved creates self-victimization. This belief can generate greed, stress, fear, integrity breakdowns, and quitting before getting started. More specifically, it stops leaders from looking to create new problems and has them playing to avoid gaps instead.

Ironically, human beings naturally look for gaps to close, challenges to overcome, and problems to solve. We create gaps for many reasons; this is quite natural. The nature of the gap will depend on the individual. Leaders create gaps on purpose in order to move forward their intended results, vision, and mission by both clearly outlining its edges and distinguishing what's in it for the team they are leading. Gaps are powerful tools in the hands of a leader. In the brink model, the mountain that leaders choose is defined by a gap that is at the same time measurable and enticing for both the leaders and their teams. This is exactly what John F. Kennedy created when he said we would put a man on the moon and bring him back safely by the end of the decade—a specific and extremely enticing gap to close.

The brink requires that a leader *intentionally* seek out a mountain and create a gap on purpose. Please remember these points about gaps:

1. There is nothing "wrong" with a gap. There are gaps in income, gaps in deadlines, and gaps in the sidewalk. We step over or close these gaps every day. We don't attach the same negative connotation to the word "gap" that we do to "problem" or "issue." Leaders know this and are intentional about relating to the space between here and there as an objective measure. Think about a long-distance trip. If you are on your way from New York to Florida, you set out mile by mile, systematically closing the gap in the distance between here and there. It's not a problem that you still have 673 miles to go but a process that will naturally unfold.

2. We instinctively close gaps. People are hard wired and intrinsically empowered to close gaps they encounter. Leaders do not need to do a great deal of convincing if a team realizes that what they are doing is closing a gap of their own choosing. Moving from where we are to where we want to be is instinctual. Think about the natural curiosity that allowed humans to discover flight and close the gap between the earth and the skies. It wasn't a problem that we couldn't fly yet, but the determination to risk inventing flight came from a gap that the Wright brothers became determined to close.

3. The gap is the whole point! A community, team, or group with a mission exists because of their commitment to closing a particular gap. That determination is the foundational reason for their decision to follow the leader. Leaders know that no matter how many followers they initially obtain, they will ultimately need to empower and inspire these followers to close a gap in order to maintain longevity and results.

Think about what happened at Ground Zero in lower Manhattan after the September 11, 2001 attacks on the World Trade Center. Firefighters and volunteer search and rescue (SAR) teams from around the world sifted and dug through rubble for weeks looking for surviving first responders and civilians, and then looking for remains when the possibility of survival diminished. The leaders of that effort knew that the gap (missing comrades) was already there and loomed large for those searching. The mission and commitment to finding survivors *created* the community of first responders who were doing the searching. It was that mission, not the site coordinator or SAR team leader, that caused them to work so tirelessly that they often had to be forced to take breaks and work in shifts. Closing this particular gap was intimately and emotionally empowered because of the nature of the tragedy that created it. The inspiration to close the gap was presented by the gap itself.

Consider also a pro football team. They follow their coach, but the coach is smart enough to keep them focused on winning the Superbowl. The gap is all the games they need to win to get there. Because they follow the leader (coach) in service of a greater gap to which they are all deeply enrolled and committed (the Superbowl), they can sustain losses, injuries, setbacks, etc. and still be effective as a team year in and year out.

In order to tackle a gap effectively, leaders can either choose a gap that already exists (e.g., armed conflict, hunger, breast cancer) or they can create one of their own (e.g., sales goal, growth plan, new engine design) and enroll a community or team in their vision of closing that gap. Leaders who are already leading teams need to ensure that their teams are addressing the right gap for the mountain they have chosen. A team that is not accustomed to climbing at steep gradients or against adversity will not likely be successful until the members are aware of what closing this particular gap means for *them*. This goes back to the importance of the vision to the mission.

Leaders who are successful on the brink will know their vision and mission the same way they know the sound of their own voice—it is a part of them, present throughout their day. In choosing a mountain to climb as their mission, leaders cannot underestimate the vital importance of having this clarity of vision present for themselves and their teams. As a business and executive coach, I have worked with many large organizations on leadership development and have regularly seen companies with their mission and vision written on a plaque on the wall that every employee walks by daily. Typically only about 20% of the employees can recite the mission and vision, and even fewer of those folks have any idea what it means, let alone how it applies to their individual everyday decision making. As such, these companies have rendered their mission and vision ineffective, and are missing out on a fundamental building block to creating leaders among their teams.

A mission and vision are only as valuable as the degree to which they are cultivated and integrated into action. For a mission and vision to be effective, leaders and those they lead must connect to it intrinsically and embody it in how they interact daily with their tasks and the roles they play. A great example of this is the U.S. military. My younger brother was a member of the 10th Mountain Infantry Unit out of Fort Benning, and was active overseas in the "global war on terror." What he shared with me was the degree to which every member of his team was powerfully reminded of its mission and vision on a consistent basis. The U.S. Army describes the mission of infantry like this: "The Infantry closes with the enemy by means of fire and maneuver in order to destroy or capture him or to repel his assault by fire, close combat, and counterattack" *(FM7-8, Infantry Rifle Platoon and Squad)*.

On a daily basis, training includes this doctrine in every aspect. Infantrymen are trained to be exceptionally well disciplined. They are developed into highly trained specialists who will continue their combat missions despite personal losses, fear, despair, fatigue, and bodily injury. This is exemplified in the U.S. Army by an excerpt from the infantryman's creed: "In the race for victory, I am swift, determined, and courageous; armed with a fierce will to win. Never will I fail my country's trust. Always I fight on: through the foe, to the objective, to triumph over all. If necessary, I fight to my death."

In other words, these men are so integrated into the mission of this country's military that they are willing to die for it. Infantrymen are not paid exceptionally well ($15-$50,000 per year) relative to the risk, but the military's leadership training and the powerful enrollment into its mission are successful—providing a good lesson for all leaders that you cannot simply pay for followers, and you do not *need* to pay for followers either.

Leadership needs to be built, not bought, and it needs to be built by you.

PICK A MOUNTAIN

CHAPTER SNAPSHOT

- The first step toward leadership on the brink is to pick a "mountain" (a goal or challenge) to which you can apply yourself, one that is bigger than you can necessarily see possible.
- Choose it in service of the leadership it will require of you to climb it.
- Fear is present on the brink of any challenging leadership possibility.
- Remember that leaders don't always look like leaders. Leadership is practiced mostly internally within a leader and only manifested externally.
- Know your vision and mission intimately.
- Regularly enroll and re-enroll the team in the vision and mission. Enrollment in the vision and mission will not last untended.
- Create new problems by moving forward and relate to them as gaps.
- Three points to remember about gaps on the brink:
  1. There is nothing "wrong" with a gap.
  2. We instinctively close gaps.
  3. The gap is the whole point!

EXERCISES/QUESTIONS

1. What is the leadership gap you see in yourself? Where have you not been a leader when you needed or wanted to be?
2. Pick *your* mountain (mission). Make sure it's bigger than any you've climbed before.
3. Mountain Board—Create a visual display of your mountain that includes the following key ingredients:
   - Specific description of the "peak" or goal
   - Measurable milestones along the way
   - Prominent placement where you will see it every day

4. What is the leadership growth you intend to create as a result of climbing the mountain to fulfill your vision?
    - What difference will it make in your life? Your work?
    - Practice identifying the gap in every "problem" you encounter and relating to it in both words and actions from that point forward as a gap.

"Nothing is so common as the wish to be remarkable."
—William Shakespeare

CHAPTER 2

KNOW THE ANSWER TO "WHAT FOR?"

ASK EARLY AND KNOW THE ANSWER

In training leaders, the question "What for?" has always been one of my favorites. I love asking the leaders I train and clients I work with what they want to take on as their mountain and then ask them flatly "What for?" What I really mean by that question is *Why bother? You are climbing this mountain in service of what? This mountain you've chosen will be hard, unsafe, and uncomfortable to climb. It will challenge you in ways you cannot possibly even predict while standing at the bottom of it here with me today. You will have to put yourself perpetually in the unknown—potentially in harm's way— and create new problems at every turn. There will be risk, adversity, and no guarantee of success.* So again, "What for?"

Without knowing the answer to the question "What for?," we are neither connected to nor willing to stick with our path when it becomes

31

inconvenient. I had this experience myself. I grew up in New York in the 70s and 80s; the lure of Wall Street was huge. I went for it. I majored in math and economics in college so I could work in finance and make the big bucks. After graduating, I worked in the reinsurance industry for over six years in New York City. (Reinsurance is an industry of companies that insure insurance companies by absorbing some of their financial risk.)

However, I discovered quickly that I had the unfortunate combination of being good at reinsurance but very unhappy in that industry. Why? I had no "What for?" other than money. Once that came in, there wasn't much else for me to get up for every day, so it became harder and harder to be good at what I did. I ended up hiring a coach as a direct result of the disconnect between what I was doing for a living and why I was doing it. Without any connection to what I was doing and no intention other than to earn good money, leadership had no place to grow within me. My commitment to nothing more than money was as shallow as it sounds.

Unhappy and complacent, I could see that I became less interested in performing at the levels I had earlier in my career. With the support of my coach, I ended up choosing to leave but was clear about two things as I left: first, that I had not truly owned my leadership in my career up until I made the decision to leave, and second, that the leaders I had worked under had not enrolled me in a vision compelling enough for me to stay.

THE BRINK IS OPTIONAL

We can place ourselves on the brink at any moment for the purpose of anything, even something that already exists or in which we are already engaged. The brink *must* start with a powerful vision and mission. From there the key is that the brink *must first be chosen before it can be generated.*

Steve Jobs changed the world and shaped the future of mobile communications as the founder and visionary mind at Apple. He did so not by enrolling you in his power and your fear. He chose a mountain to climb that was so appealing that others wanted to climb it with him just to belong to it and be a part of it. He did so by getting people to see that they *needed* a phone that was "smart," played music, and had an "app for everything." Cell phones were already common; Jobs made them indispensable, and he made you his ally in doing so.

The truth is that not all mountains are arduous and painful to climb. Jobs and Apple make much more than computers, iPods, and phones. They create a communal brink for us as consumers in the mountain they have chosen for themselves. They make us think about what's possible every time we pick up our phones. They make us anticipate, predict, and collaborate with them in what's next. *That* is leadership on the brink: creating followers who are enrolled, loyal, and in love with each part of the vision, including the next iteration of it.

An entire genre of electronics came from the iPhone. The "smart phone" has been replicated by other companies trying to cash in on the revolution caused by Jobs, but none have created anywhere near the same following of committed fans and consumers that he has. Jobs saw what we wanted to see, gave us a peek, and then gave us access for a price that was extravagant but worth it for the possibility of belonging. Genius! (Pun intended.)

"What for?" is an imperative question for leaders on the brink to ask—of themselves *and* their followers, because whether they ask out loud or not, everyone else is already thinking it and wondering. Leaders on the brink need to normalize this question and not be surprised by it.

THE FOUR BIGGEST ANSWERS TO THE QUESTION "WHAT FOR?"

As a leader on the brink, you'll find it valuable to know some of the answers you are likely to get to this question, since you will be asking it so frequently. Here are the four most common answers to that question, in order of prevalence:

1. Money
2. Security
3. Service
4. Well-being

It's worth looking at these options first in order to integrate the vision and mission in which you are intending to enroll people with at least one of these answers, but do not be fooled by this list. People can be motivated by anything they choose, and you can enroll them in anything if you are willing and they are enrollable. This list is simply a summary of the most common responses to the question.

What motivates people differs, but in order to effectively lead a team, all members must get the connection between the mountain and the thing they most want in the world. The job of leaders on the brink is to uncover and distinguish that connection with their team.

WHY > WHAT > HOW

As we just discussed, the first and most vital question for followers is **why** they are climbing this mountain with the leader. This question is answered in the vision the leader has put forth, which (as we stated earlier) needs to be reiterated regularly so that the team stays conscious of it. The second most important question is **what** mountain they will be climbing. This is clearly outlined in the missions leaders generate, and it defines the brink itself— the mountain/challenge they will undertake in service of the vision. The third and least important is the **how**. Unfortunately, many leaders make the mistake of starting from this place. The answer to the question "**How** will we climb this mountain?" is typically not easy to answer, because it is not 100% clear at the outset. Typically there is no predictable path outlined when the leader sets the mission.

However, after enrolling a team in the why and then the what, the question "How?" becomes almost inconsequential. By the time team members are enrolled in the why and what, they are typically willing to work out the how along the way, and even collaborate in its creation themselves! This is the primary reason that leaders on the brink need to be aware of which questions are answered in what order. Using the proper hierarchy of questions will facilitate moving their team of followers up the mountain through the many challenges and in service of the answer to "How?" It will also make present in every step they take along the way the reason they are there.

CONTEXT

The brink is a paradigm shift. It requires us to literally look at our mountain through a completely different paradigm or lens. A paradigm is a way of looking at things that includes our beliefs and assumptions. If the current paradigm is determined to be insufficient or ineffective, then using a new paradigm is what allows us to infinitely expand the range of what we produce on the brink. A paradigm shift is not a slightly different version but a quantum leap.

In order to shift a paradigm, as leaders we must be able to gain "altitude" on the current one in place. Here, altitude means a higher level of perspective that allows us to be able to see the many variables in our paradigm at once. With altitude, we can see more of the landscape, including the paradigm we have been operating from and the value of choosing another. Sometimes, in order to answer the question "What for?" sufficiently, we need to gain that altitude and shift our paradigm, or that of our team. Shifting our paradigm increases our options exponentially and creates the opportunity to generate more power than if we did not look at all.

The context in which a team relates to the mountain the leader has identified will define the success of the team, vision, and mission itself. That context has everything to do with success when there is adversity. By default, people tend to focus on and try to fix what isn't working in the face of adversity by looking at the component parts or ingredients. Typically we look for the piece that is broken or the components that are misplaced and move them around, hoping that the solution to the "problem" lies in addressing these issues.

What if you planned a big vacation by focusing all your attention on how bad traffic would be, how long the lines at the airport would be, how bad the food on the plane would be, and how far you'd have to go to get there. Sound like fun? Focusing on problems and avoiding adversity doesn't help empower or move forward any goal, yet we do the very same thing with our businesses, dreams, and lives every day. We create a big goal and then begin to strategize, reformulate, change players, add or subtract ingredients—all in an attempt to avoid the full experience of the journey and the mountain itself. We think that the secret to being successful lies in the details, in fixing the content of what we are trying to do.

Here's the key to the city: the actual solution—and the only sustainable one—lies in shifting your and your team's **context**. Think of your context as the paradigm or filter through which you view the world (or a specific aspect of it). Everything you see, all the content you ever come across is filtered through that context—*all* of it.

I like to think of context like a pair of blue tinted sunglasses you walk around wearing at all times. Everything you see will appear to you as some shade of blue. No one will be able to convince you that the room you are standing in is not painted blue. This is the equivalent of how most of us approach problem solving or success in reaching a large goal—by addressing the surroundings and the content of the room. "It's all blue. We need to repaint" (or clean the walls, or buy better quality paint next time, or hire a consultant to pick a color that isn't blue, or move to a new building, or convince the world that everything's blue, or decide that we just have to live with it and manage around it...).

Doesn't make a whole lot of sense, does it? Yet this is what people, corporations, and leaders all over the world do every day. Working on content and not context shows up in the corporation that fires and replaces employees continuously when results aren't produced. It shows up in the business owner who changes suppliers and contractors regularly, hopelessly looking for the right combination of ingredients that will finally produce the results. It shows up in employees who work harder and harder every time they are passed over for promotion. It even shows up in people who repeatedly argue with their significant others about something that so bothers them.

All these instances are examples of addressing the paint on the walls, the furniture in the room, and the quality of the paint job—completely ignoring the blue tinted sunglasses, the filter itself. How instead would things occur if you understood that you were wearing those blue tinted sunglasses, *that you were actually looking and taking actions through a filter*? What if you also discovered that you have a choice about wearing those glasses?

Here's what's possible:

- You could choose a new filter or none at all—a whole new context from which to operate.
- You could take back your power and ability to create sustained change and reinvention.
- You could finally achieve that result that has often eluded you when the old ineffective filter was in place.

Individuals, groups, organizations, corporations, governments, and nations all operate out of *some* context or filter. Many operate out of a context of fear and cultivate that culture from the top down and the inside out. Alternatively, some operate from one of scarcity; no matter how much is accumulated or gained, it will never be enough. Others operate from a context of abundance and 100% ownership of their experience, actions, and results. That context will be directly reflected in their experience, actions, and results.

Choosing a new filter is the single point in any process, goal, or project that can be instantly shifted to create fundamental and systemic change, both in the process and in the success of the result. The brink requires this as part of the leader's process. It requires that a leader be responsible for being aware of and shifting the team's context as needed. The best part isn't just that it's easy. It's that once the new context has been identified and sufficiently integrated, the success of the individual, group, or corporation tends to be permanent. A new context creates a fundamental shift with lasting results that permeate the business or relationship. This type of change can then be propagated throughout the organization or the life of the individual. Just as a bad habit or addiction will affect all parts of a project or individual's life, so will a context.

Leaders on the brink do not just address content. We often don't even need to hear the story or the details. We focus on the context, the filter through which the results and details are being realized. We identify that context inside and out. Then we give ourselves and our teams the choice of what comes next.

CONTROLLED FALLS

I had a theoretical mathematics professor in college who described the act of walking in a way that made a profound difference for me. He redefined walking as nothing more than a "controlled fall"—and he proved it. Think about it: If you become present to taking the next step as you walk, what you're really doing is shifting your weight forward to the point of imbalance. That then requires you to respond by putting one foot out in front in order to catch yourself. And then you do it again with the other foot. Running is just a sped-up version of this.

This new way of looking at something as basic as walking through the hyper-present lens of *creating an imbalance so as to propel ourselves forward* has stayed with me. It became a mantra of mine and inspired me to redefine imbalance and discomfort as an access point to propulsion. I also was astonished at the level of presence it takes to recognize something like this. Some things are buried in plain sight within an action we all do daily! This is context awareness and shifting at their core—relating to a familiar thing in an unfamiliar and even curious way. The millions of things we do each day become meaningless for us unless we are present to the possibility that they are more than we currently realize.

Leaders on the brink are fully responsible for being aware of this and making sure we regularly practice being present and curious about the lens we are looking through. We must lead from the front and contextualize challenges and adversities in a way that empowers and engages our teams. On the brink, there is no space for the mission and vision to go stale and the team to get lazy in relating to any of it as "rote."

THE BALANCE MYTH

In this conversation about "What for?" and controlled falls, let's consider balance. People talk about balance, motivational speakers and self-help books tell people how to find it, and we all believe that we want it (mostly because it sounds good). But I regularly train leaders to stop looking for balance. It's the last thing leaders actually want or need.

Think about it: Imbalance is what creates forward momentum. Balance creates stillness. Imbalance causes us to have to adjust and grow so we can move forward. Balance must be maintained in a delicate set of circumstances that are inconsistent by nature.

Leaders must not only learn to accept imbalance but also go so far as to intentionally generate it in order to stimulate growth and possibilities that were absent when balance was present. When building new muscle in the gym, we put our bodies in positions that are intentionally out of balance and force them to compensate, thus generating growth. If we leave any muscle in a state of "balance," it simply atrophies over time or gets good at only a narrow set of movements that are simply limited.

Leading a team is no different. We need not only to celebrate imbalance but also seek it out in service of the growth of the team and the goal. As with the controlled fall we discussed earlier, imbalance actually causes us to activate our natural instincts to search out balance again, and it is *that* natural instinct and rebalancing that creates new muscle and new opportunities.

The brink requires of the leader who has chosen the mountain and the team that will follow an awareness, facility, comfort, and intentionality around imbalance. Imbalance is actually a tool that serves the climb up the mountain we have chosen, because it has us continually reestablish an empowered relationship with the answer to "What for?" Being continually put off balance by our mission requires us again and again to adapt, grow, and reconnect to why we are taking on all this effort and challenge, in order to continue. Imbalance itself is part of the attraction of doing something new and difficult. Consider learning to ride a bicycle. Imbalance teaches us body awareness that has us able to adapt to the wheels, pedals, and terrain moving rapidly beneath us. When we fall, we learn. We also scrape our knees and elbows, so we have to re-establish the reason we wanted to learn to ride this contraption in the first place before choosing to get back on it and risk falling again. This reconnection to the answer to "What for?" solidifies our relationship to it and deepens our resolve over time.

PAYOFF

Whenever my clients get stuck in a familiar pattern that is getting in their way, I ask them a question that tends to surprise them: "What's the *payoff* you get from this pattern?" This question is often difficult for people to grasp, mostly because the pattern and results they are seeing are ones that they do *not* like or want. As a result, they cannot imagine that they are getting a payoff from the pattern. But the truth is they would not be creating this pattern if there were no payoff. Yes, even if they disagree or cannot see anything positive from it, they are getting *something* from its repetition, even if it hurts. They are most likely either doing it because it's comfortable or familiar, they fear the consequences of not doing it, or they are so practiced at it that they are unaware of it.

The payoff might be familiarity with an old story about failure, getting to be right about how hard things are, reinforcing the story they have about being "too busy," or simply getting to delay until later what would be uncomfortable today. The *game* they are playing is what is faulty—not the pattern or results. They are simply suffering from an old familiar strategy that has them achieving an unintentional payoff that sabotages them at the same time.

As a leader on the brink, you need to know what the payoffs are in your game and your team's game. If you know them, then you can either change the game, interrupt it, or capitalize on it intentionally. Effectively using the brink as a catalyst for change, generating leadership, and creating breakthrough results requires not just new action but also a whole new relationship to the game we are playing and mountain we are climbing. It requires a context shift such that we embody a propensity for risk, discomfort, and unfamiliarity in a way that actually supports the "What for" we have created. This is the same way that skydivers embody a context that *includes* risk, discomfort, and unfamiliarity that supports their commitment to the rush of jumping out of a perfectly sound airplane—otherwise, they would never jump. In other words, the brink requires us to relate to risk, discomfort, and unfamiliarity in a way that has us no longer focus on avoiding any of these experiences. In this way, we can instead focus on the task at hand: reaching the summit.

This is similar to the way in which rescue divers must normalize their work environment in order to do their jobs underwater. Their context shifts to one of normality in the face of dozens of dangers that are present in every moment that they are submerged. With that all normalized, they can get to work rescuing those in need of help. Remember, nothing you have ever created of any consequence would have been described at its outset as "safe, comfortable, and familiar," right?

DYING BEFORE GOING INTO BATTLE

The Samurai warriors of ancient Japan would famously "die before going into battle"—not literally, of course, but figuratively. They believed that the warrior needed to fully accept his death before entering battle so that the focus in battle was victory, not survival. By having already accepted their deaths, the Samurai were able to fight without fear of dying.

Leadership requires this same level of commitment and choice. The possibility of failure has already presented itself, because without climbing the mountain, the vision and mission are dead before taking a single step. But once that vision and mission have been declared, you no longer need to fear failing. The possibility of climbing and failing is no worse than the tragedy that not living your vision would be.

You cannot conquer anything that you do not first acknowledge exists, including the possibility of failure. Once you accept that failure exists as a possibility, you can plan to conquer it. This is a major reason that people avoid declaring a vision and mission—because they fear failure so much that they avoid acknowledging its possibility or risking it at all.

On the brink, on the other hand, leaders hold their vision and mission in this context—they normalize the possibility of failure to the extent that they are focused on the mission without worrying about what might happen. In their eyes, the possibility of failure is already present, and they are simply focused on the possibility of success *instead*. As a leader on the brink, you must be as well. There is no room here for spending time and energy worrying about failing.

REVERENCE

The brink and reverence are inextricably linked. Reverence is a deep respect for something or someone—the experience of awe. At the brink, we experience reverence, a powerful respect for and relationship to something greater than ourselves. On the brink, leaders revere their vision, their mission (the mountain), and their followers. Reverence can be said to be the "What for?" behind the "What for?"

In his book *Reverence*, Paul Woodruff states, "Leadership does not serve small goals any more than reverence stands in awe of small things …" and relates to "irreverence as the plainest clue to tyranny…. Shared reverence is the mark of good leaders and their followers." Reverence inspires the manner in which a leader's vision and mission are executed. It paves the path and instills each action and collaboration with integrity and meaning. Leaders on the brink practice reverence in their lives as well as in their professional missions. This includes their work, physical existence, relationships, and spirituality. The brink requires that leaders be aware of the systemic effect of reverence and honor its significance in all parts of their experiences.

PARITY

The word "parity" comes from the Latin root *par*, meaning "equal." On the brink, there is parity in leadership. Hierarchy has no place here. Leaders operating on the brink do not need to be "above" their followers or position themselves as "better than" anyone in any way. In fact, the greatest leaders on the brink do not look to create followers at all; *they look to create and surround themselves with other leaders*. These leaders know that this type of parity helps partnership between team members evolve more powerfully, allowing team members to be more empowered and invested.

These leaders also know that creating followers who are leaders themselves means that these "follower leaders" may at times be unwilling to obey, and this is not only acceptable but also necessary. The rebels and free spirits on a team who see things in a different paradigm often make the greatest innovative contributions. The integrity of the vision and mission requires an occasional dissenter in the ranks—someone willing to go against the grain. Parity allows for the value in all of this to be seen, heard, and integrated. Parity compels team members to relate to one another and themselves powerfully as leaders with responsibility and influence. This level playing field means no one is waiting for someone else to lead her/him or to say that s/he is a leader.

Three characteristics of a leader generate parity on the brink:

1. **Relationship to Self (Being).** Leaders on the brink must have an empowered and solid relationship to themselves in order to play with parity on their team.
2. **Connection to the Team (Influence).** The leader on the brink must be strongly connected to the team and invested in their success and the success of their individual members. This investment will create relationships that will weather all storms and empower parity.
3. **Strength of Spirit (Faith).** Leaders on the brink must embody faith in order to step out of old force-based hierarchical leadership models and into one of parity. They much have faith in themselves, the team, and the vision.

These are the core of what is needed to create parity.

When these three ingredients are aligned with vision and mission, leaders can most effectively own the mountain they have chosen and empower the leaders around them to partner most effectively in climbing it. Structurally aligning these aspects of your being with your vision, mission, and life in general gives you access to power on the brink. The alignment of one's life with one's greatest goals creates a foundation on which the biggest endeavors can be undertaken solidly.

Parity is an important part of the answer to the question "What for?" With parity we find the grace and power we need in the team we have created. Reaching the peak of the mountain no longer appears the only goal; the manner in which we get there starts to matter, because we care about the team and its experience of the climb itself as well. This level of parity is not fragile. On the contrary, it is resilient. Practiced consistently, it can create inherent upward movement as the mountain is climbed. On the brink, parity is a key ingredient in giving juice to the vision and mission, because it allows the team members to relate to each as their own.

KNOW THE ANSWER TO "WHAT FOR?"

CHAPTER SNAPSHOT

- Know the answer to "What For?" for yourself and for your team.
  - The four most popular answers to "What For?":
    1. Money
    2. Security
    3. Service
    4. Well-being
- Remember that the brink is a choice, and you must continue to relate to it that way.
- Why > What > How
  - Address these questions in this order for yourself and your team.
    - ◊ Focus on context over content. Context will create bigger, longer-lasting results.
    - ◊ Stop looking for balance. As a leader, it does not serve you.
      - In fact, leaders on the brink *seek out* imbalances as access to growth.
- The patterns of breakdown you typically experience give you a payoff.
  - If you are repeating the pattern, then you are getting something out of it.
  - Know the pattern and the payoff so that you can choose whether to keep it or change it.
- The brink requires reverence—reverence for the team, vision, and mission (mountain).
- Parity is a tool of leadership on the brink. It creates ownership in each team member, as well as a team of leaders rather than just followers.
  - There are three qualities of a leader that are key to creating parity:

1. Relationship to Self (Being)
2. Connection to Team (Influence)
3. Strength of Spirit (Faith)

EXERCISES/QUESTIONS

1. List the top five "mountains" (goals) you have in your life and work.
   - For each, identify the following:
     o What is your "What For?"
     o What is the main context you have around each? (Consider your beliefs and assumptions about this that are contributing to your not having achieved it yet.)
     o Identify one imbalance (way of getting out of your comfort zone) that would spur growth in that area.
       ◊ Create that imbalance in each, one at a time.
     o What was the payoff to the breakdown that most recently occurred in each area?
     o Rate yourself on a scale of 1-10 in each of the three measures of parity for each mountain:
       ◊ Relationship to Self (Being)
       ◊ Connection to Team (Influence)
       ◊ Strength of Spirit (Faith)
2. You now have a list of these components for each mountain you are climbing.
   - Keep this list with you and read it at least once a week.
     o Use it as a living document for 30 consecutive days.
     o Update it regularly and work to improve upon your performance in each area.

"We are each on our own journey. Each of us is on our very own adventure, encountering all kinds of challenges, and the choices we make on that adventure will shape us as we go; these choices will stretch us, test us and push us to our limit; and our adventure will make us stronger than we ever knew we could be."
—Aamnah Akram

CHAPTER 3

CHOOSE EVERYTHING

CROSSROADS

The brink is a **crossroads**. Choice is present with every step. In each moment, you have a choice between the old, familiar way and a new path.

The brink challenges leaders to practice putting themselves at crossroads and making choices at every moment. Every misstep, challenge, win, and setback—every possible experience you may encounter—is of your own choosing once you've selected a mountain to climb.

Choice opens the way for more acceptance of whatever might come your way and is ultimately the key to any significant undertaking as a leader. It allows access to both power and enrollment; people will follow the clarity and decisiveness in powerful choices all the way. Choice at this level removes the context of doubt. It eliminates conversations about what to do next and questions about whether the next step is the best one or worth the risk. Choice positions leaders and their teams as *all in.*

Choice is inescapable on the brink. Think about this like parachuting. When you strap on your parachute and jump from the open door of an airplane, every foot you fall and every possible outcome that unfolds from there develops out of the initial choice to leap. The events that follow are themselves choices that were inherent in the fundamental choice to jump.

With choice, there is no victimization. With choice, there is absolute ownership of every step. With choice, you keep focus when a setback occurs. With choice, there is only acceptance, adaptation, and innovation in the face of the challenges that arise.

The ability to choose is one of the greatest natural and inherent gifts we are given, yet most people are unaware of its value and power, and thereby end up either squandering it or being victimized by it. You may have noticed that most people don't live consciously aware of the choices they are making—of either that they are making them or that they are being impacted by the choices they have made. Most people think about life as something that is happening to them, and many complain about how unfair it all is.

Many people make a point of fighting for the right to have and make choices but then fail to exercise this right fully once they have it. It's easier to complain about not having choice than it is to own that everything is a choice and to choose responsibly. Leaders should be acutely aware of this habit and the commonly limited interpretation of choice as "the right to have options." The truth is that choice *also* includes the responsibility to both make and empower our choices, which means being responsible for the fact that every circumstance we encounter gives us a choice, and being responsible for the consequences of each choice we make or don't make. In fact, most people don't even realize the nature of their relationship to choice; as a thing they feel they should have, even while they are, in fact, uncomfortable choosing.

On the brink, leaders get to choose and empower others' choices as well. As coaches, we place clients at crossroads of choice all the time. We hold people accountable to their goals in the face of their greatest fears until they consciously choose to either continue to engage in an old fear-based pattern or to go down a new path.

CHALLENGE PATTERNS

All leaders have what I call a "challenge pattern," a specific, habitual routine they go through in making a decision when faced with a challenge. In the most dire circumstances, leaders will follow an individual pattern that is all their own. Leaders are well served by becoming aware of this challenge pattern they use to address difficult choices and challenges. Here are some commonalities found most often among leaders' challenge patterns:

1. **Options**—First, leaders weigh their options, or in the absence of predetermined options, generate the options from which they will choose.

2. **Consequences**—Next, leaders weigh the consequences of each of their options and the consequences of choosing them.

3. **Fear**—The fear of choice will be present throughout the process and strongest at the point of choosing. This stage is most uncomfortable and also most crucial for leaders on the brink to expect and move through.

4. **Choice**—This is where a decision is made, and either success or catastrophe becomes possible. This is precisely where leaders on the brink thrive most. This is the point of no return.

5. **Action**—The final stage is action. Action is often taken too early (or even first), before a clear direction has been determined or powerful choices made.

The symbol for chaos in Chinese is the same as the symbol for opportunity. The chaos that results from a challenge and having to generate options and then choose one goes along with the opportunity. The leader on the brink is keenly aware of this and uses it as a tool for reinvention and momentum.

On the brink, once the challenge pattern is completed and a foundational choice is made, there is no going back. This is great news! It's actually easier from here. The plane door has been opened, you are strapped into your parachute, and you have jumped. From there, falling to earth is simply not optional anymore. The choice point is the place on the brink where change is imminent.

You can buy and buy into countless leadership training programs and how-to books on the market. Most are the opinions of those who have the title of "leader" and are sharing their stories, and some are the result of study and research of others' leadership. Consider this: Before all this expertise arrived on the scene, did leaders exist? Where were they trained? Abraham Lincoln, Rosa Parks, Winston Churchill, the Dalai Lama, Indira Gandhi, Martin Luther King Jr., Madeline Albright, etc. These are some of the most memorable names in history, and these people were leaders before the "how-to revolution" took place or the research was done. In fact, most contemporary leadership research references *them* as examples of leadership.

What made them leaders before they were told how? It's simple: They *chose* leadership. Some had it thrust upon them, some sought it out, but either way, at some point they had a challenge and a choice, and they chose to own their leadership. Choice is the single most powerful aspect in developing one's leadership. Once the choice is made, the path becomes illuminated, and new options arise that did not previously seem to exist.

STANDING OVATIONS

I've noticed something over the years about standing ovations in crowded theaters. Yes, they're powerful moments that provide the opportunity to celebrate greatness, but there's also a leadership component to the standing ovation. Of the people in the audience engaging in the standing ovation, if you watch closely, there are very specific groups that self-define:

- About 5% initiate the standing ovation because they are inspired/moved and willing to express it, calling forth their fellow crowd members.
- About 45% want to stand but, out of fear of embarrassment, are waiting for someone else to stand first. They follow the initial 5%.
- About 45% don't want to stand but even more so don't want to be left out, so they hesitantly stand next.

- About 5% are angry at feeling pressured to stand, so they either stay seated or stand begrudgingly and/or out of obligation.

What this means is that if you walk into an auditorium in the middle of a standing ovation, you will see leaders and followers acting out their roles in real time. It is also important to know that they've each chosen the specific role they will take on in those moments before they ever got there in that room together; they will respond to the standing ovation based on that choice to be a visible instigator of the celebration or to be a follower of others in it, if at all. Why does this matter? Because you get to say which of these groups you will be in before you walk into another performance. You get to go do so in life, too—at work, on your team, in your office, in front of that room full of followers. You get to either be an initiator and a leader who chooses to stand or a resentful clapper who stands or stays seated because s/he feels coerced.

NOT CHOOSING

Refusing or waiting to make a choice is a choice itself. The unfortunate truth, though, is that not choosing is typically a choice that you would not consciously make on purpose. Whether you make a choice or not, something will happen, and consequences will unfold, either designed by you or for you. Not choosing is an express lane trip to being victimized by a choice that ultimately gets made for you.

Leaders on the brink know this well and do not avoid or delay choices any longer than necessary. Not choosing is not a viable option for those climbing a mountain. Choices there need to be made and empowered quickly and confidently, with a willingness to live with the consequences. Leaders on the brink are committed to making those consequences be ones they have chosen.

UNCONDITIONAL CURIOSITY

Curiosity is one of the most important assets of leaders. Curiosity invites innovation, collaboration, investigation, and growth. On the brink, it is an absolute requirement for leadership. Unconditional curiosity separates great leaders from ineffective ones. For them, curiosity is authentic, not chosen for convenience.

Unconditional curiosity is one of the most potent tools a leader can wield, and also, unfortunately, one of the most rare. It's much easier to simply rely on a familiar pattern and evidence from the past than it is to get curious and innovate. The brink requires that leaders choose curiosity as the basis on which to move forward. Curiosity creates possibility by its very nature; curiosity has us see possibility that otherwise would not be considered at all.

PAIN

Pain is a funny thing. It is a large part of most processes, and yet most of us avoid it at all costs. Those of us who have experienced it deeply or for prolonged periods know that it can become both familiar and even a welcome sign of growth and expansion. Pain reminds us that we are alive, in the middle of transforming, healing, or giving birth to something new and wonderful.

Leaders on the brink do not avoid pain and discomfort. They move into them, using their pain and discomfort as signposts along the path up their mountain. They expect and normalize both as invaluable, unavoidable indicators of their leadership in action.

Unfortunately, the entire construct of our culture is designed to flatten our risk and dampen our experience of any pain at all, as well as to extend that dulled version of ourselves for as long as possible. The design of this is inherently numbing in its attempt to protect us both from ourselves and from the world around us. This endangers the foundation of leadership.

Focusing on protecting ourselves or dulling discomfort dissuades us from putting ourselves on the brink in the first place. This construct creates comfort and complacency in a leadership system that was naturally created in—and has thrived on—uncertainty, adversity, and innovation. It creates, instead, the illusion of control and constancy in a world that is changing and evolving in every moment. No constancy exists for leaders except the constancy of change. "Job security" and "safety" are illusions; there are no guarantees. And pain and discomfort are inherently part of our lives.

Who we choose to be when faced with pain is a crucial choice for us as leaders. How we hold pain, the lengths we go to avoid it, the relationship we have with it—friendly or hostile ... These are all choices. As leaders, we are always up to creating *something* new. Pain is a partner in our growth on that brink. Ask a fitness professional—we literally need to tear muscle fiber in order for muscle to grow. It hurts. People in the know both expect and welcome this as part of the process of building muscle and strength.

Our culture intervenes in our growth and protects us from the very thing—making leadership choices that will lead to experiences of growth and pain—that would propel us forward most powerfully. Growth is inherently painful in big choices that will have us experience change, like starting a company, investing in new equipment or resources, or stepping into leadership on a team. The edge of the brink is not comfortable or safe, and our belief that we don't need or want to risk the experience of pain is our greatest undoing. Leaders know this, and they choose to thrive on pain and discomfort. They not only pull back the veil on the illusion, but they actually seek out that edge, that discomfort, the pain that defines the growth they are compelled to undertake.

Leaders live and play on the brink with reverence alongside the fear and pain. You can too. You simply need to stop avoiding your pain and discomfort and relating to them as "enemies." A true appreciation of the brink doesn't ignore or try to avoid pain; it recognizes it along with all the other contradictions, ingredients, and complexities of growth. This part of the process on the brink must not be avoided—not because it is pleasant or easy but because it is part of your growth and development as a leader as you make your way to the top of your mountain.

CHOOSE EVERYTHING

CHAPTER SNAPSHOT

- The brink is a continual crossroads. Leaders there need to constantly acknowledge that they have a choice, choose, and move forward.
- Choices up the mountain are all part of the initial choice to climb the mountain in the first place.
  - Like parachuting out of an airplane, every foot you fall and the consequences of the fall are part of the choice to jump in the first place.
  - Challenge patterns are the unique patterns each leader follows when faced with a challenge, and include the following common stages:
    1. *Options*
    2. *Consequences*
    3. *Fear*
    4. *Choice*
    5. *Action*
  - Not choosing is a choice that leaves you victimized when a choice gets made for you unintentionally.
  - Pain is an unavoidable part of leadership and growth and is something that the leader on the brink both normalizes and embraces.

EXERCISES/QUESTIONS

1. List the three most recent big choices you have made.
   - Now list the three most recent big choices you have avoided.
   - What is the difference you notice in the outcome of the three you chose vs. the three you avoided?
2. Identify and write out your own personal challenge pattern.
   - The next time you are challenged by something, take it out and read this. Notice how closely and naturally you follow that pattern.

- Make changes to the written version so that the pattern serves you better as a leader the next time you are challenged.
- Keep this as a living document, a pattern that you will continually be making changes to and fine tuning.

3. Make a list of the top 10 places you avoid pain in your goals/life.
   - Practice moving toward and allowing the pain in each area (where physically safe to do so).
   - What do you notice is the difference in the experience and the outcome of moving into that pain rather than away from it?

"Try again. Fail again. Fail better."
—Samuel Beckett

CHAPTER 4

PRACTICE

WHAT *IS* PRACTICE?

Buddhist teachings call for *right practice* as the access point to ceasing all suffering. The definition of right practice is important for our practice of leadership on the brink, as it informs *how* we practice as much as it does *that* we practice. The translation of the original Sanskrit into "right" is misleading here. The word Buddhists use is actually translated from Sanskrit more accurately as "complete, together, coherent, wholesome."

This is how leaders must practice on the brink. Here, practice is everything, and everything is practice. There is no arrival, no perfection. There is only more practice and the further learning that arises. Practice *is* the way.

Our relationship to practice is key here. If we look at how most people relate to practice, it's easy to understand why leadership is so rare. Most people avoid practice because it's uncomfortable, and it doesn't look good either to others or to oneself while engaged in it.

An alternate, empowering notion of practice creates much more room in which to stretch, learn, challenge ourselves, and grow both as leaders and members of a team. Relate to practice like it's the whole point, the end, and the means all in one. The *real* question is, "Are you willing to give up performing in the short term in order to 'just' practice?"

THE SIX PRINCIPLES OF PRACTICE ON THE BRINK

There are six fundamental principles of practice, which, when present, produce the most powerful and effective results for both leader and team on the brink:

1. **Persistence**—The most effective practice is persistent practice. A leader must be relentless in order to practice in a way that yields rich, lasting, and productive results.

2. **Intentionality**—Practice must be taken on intentionally. It must be given the same reverence as the performance in which we are so often engaged and must be planned, scheduled, and executed for a specific purpose each time. This creates both focus and power in practice.

3. **Urgency**—Creating urgency in practice generates stretching of boundaries and limits. Urgency is not just about time but also about desire and the generation of energy. Establishing urgency as part of practice makes it a more effective tool for growth.

4. **Curiosity**—One of the keys to effective practice is curiosity. It forces us to step outside the familiar and innovate. Curiosity provides access to greater learning, growth, and creativity, all of which allow us to become more effective at what we are practicing and at our practice itself.

5. **Commitment**—Commitment is essential to practice. It keeps us on track, has us continue to practice even when we don't "feel like it," and generates enrollment, both in leaders and in those they lead. Commitment is effectively the backbone of practice in that the thing you are committed to is also the answer to the question

"What for?", and your practice of it is what causes your leadership to grow and the mountain to be climbed.

6. **Play**—This is perhaps the most important component of effective practice. Play allows us to be unattached, natural, and fully expressed as part of our leadership. It makes practice fun! Finding ways to incorporate play into practice will unlock other principles of practice and create energy, ease, and flow along the way.

PERFORMANCE

Practice and performance are very different entities on the brink. Typically we confuse the two and expect to perform when we actually are intending to practice. This causes discouragement, mostly because we have impossible expectations of ourselves. The reason we practice is so that we can perform later and not the other way around. Unfortunately, reason doesn't play much of a role in our need to perform and "look good" to ourselves and others.

In his book *Outliers*, Malcolm Gladwell addresses what he calls the "10,000 hour rule." This rule effectively states that in order to relate to ourselves as experts in our field and to truly perform at our top level, we need to first practice the specific task for at least 10,000 hours. Leaders on the brink know this intimately and are less interested in being related to as an expert than they are in practicing so as to produce results.

Leadership requires risk. Practice comes with plenty of it—the risk of looking bad, experiencing failure, and becoming discouraged, among others. Practice actually creates a safe place for risk to exist. In practice, we fully *expect* to fail repeatedly. Practice gives us permission to take risks, swing in new directions, and miss completely. It gives us permission to free ourselves from the constraints of having to perform and allows us to make mistakes on the practice field that we will not need to make later while performing.

Leaders must be able to adapt, take risks, and innovate while performing at their highest levels. What practice actually provides is a comfort level with future practice *while* performing. Then when we are performing and something goes not as we intended, we are able to respond using the muscle memory we have developed from all that prior practice. In other words, leaders on the brink know that practice does not end, even while performing; it simply becomes integrated into our performance.

Leadership on this level is most effectively practiced when the stakes are high. Practice in the face of risk stretches and encourages us to be adaptable in the moment. Practicing solely within safe spaces, where there is nothing at stake, is akin to practicing tightrope walking on a line in the sidewalk but never raising ourselves even an inch off the floor. Leadership is not effectively developed if we confine ourselves to what's comfortable and safe.

THE COMFORT MYTH

On the brink, comfort is a trap. The task of leaders on the brink is to know that comfort will not likely be present, to be wary of when and where it is present, and to get comfortable with their own and others' discomfort. Discomfort is simply another place for leaders on the brink to practice and become familiar with their own edges.

One of the things I love about practicing sports, particularly CrossFit, is that it never gets easier. No matter how strong or good you get, you must constantly move into places where you are less comfortable as you compete against yourself and the clock. And the best part is that you never run out of those places, and this becomes a source of unlimited growth. The growth is unlimited in that it gets harder as you get better at it—by design. The thing you are really getting better at is *practicing*.

An empowered relationship with practice and discomfort is a gift. You develop power in your relationship with discomfort by practicing it, and the best way to achieve that is to simply stop avoiding it. Instead, start seeking it out. *Look for* the places and challenges that scare you, that you avoid, and that you work so hard to mitigate. Start taking them on and stepping directly toward them. Make the discomfort familiar, and it quickly becomes a guide.

On the brink, discomfort will be an absolutely necessary ally and guide. The ability to "be with" discomfort means that you are willing to be in its presence and move forward through it without avoiding it. It's essential for leaders to *allow* discomfort to be present. Understanding this is what enables leaders to navigate the unknown without requiring it look a certain way, be comfortable, or seem familiar. This is crucial because, after all, familiarity and comfort do not exist on the unknown side of your mountain.

STOP PLANNING PICNICS BASED ON THE WEATHER

A favorite saying of mine is "Stop planning picnics based on the weather." Leaders on the brink need to plan their proverbial picnics, or mountain ascents, based on their intentions and commitments, not on what might happen adversely. Rain, wind, and fog will happen. Predicting them is a rough science at best.

Weathermen are the only professionals I know of who are wrong most of the time and still keep their jobs. We even know they're wrong, but we still listen to them and plan around their predictions. Why? Because they give us a sense of control or knowledge in a part of life where neither is actually possible. Nevertheless, checking the forecast makes us feel safe, no matter how falsely.

Leaders on the brink don't worry about the proverbial "weather forecast." Their plans are based on commitments too big to be at the mercy of chance. The picnic will happen, rain or shine. We may get wet, it may be windy, and the visibility may be low, but that's not the only point of the picnic. The bigger picture is the commitment that the plan served in the first place. In a business, the bigger picture is typically the bottom line, and the "weather" we encounter along the way (the economy, interest rates, employee turnover, competitor underpricing, etc.) does not deter leaders from their focus on that bottom line. They still expect that the goal be reached, regardless of the adversity that arises, so the focus is on the proverbial "picnic" itself, not the weather forecast.

Leaders take the reins of what will transpire and bring it into existence using their own actions. They bring an umbrella *and* plan to get wet. Whatever happens along the way merely offers opportunity to practice adaptation and innovation. Emerging circumstances and adversity stop being things to avoid or reasons to cancel a picnic and start being places to grow and opportunities on which to capitalize.

CLUTCH

In sports, top performers tend to be referred to as "clutch." In other words, when the game is on the line, they can be relied on to pull through, perform at the highest levels, and generate what it takes to win. What most casual observers don't realize is that these players are not only still practicing but they are also playing in a way that is actually disengaged from winning in the moment. Leaders on the brink must be able to focus on the next step in their process in order to win, which requires them not to focus on winning itself, but on *what comes next en route* to winning. Catching the ball in the end zone, getting the next corporate deal completed, throwing the next strike, hitting the three-pointer at the buzzer, leading a team through adversity in its darkest hours ... These are all times when leaders are surprisingly focused the *least* on performing and the *most* on practicing, being creative, adapting, being flexible, and shifting as their path unfolds before them. Being clutch is simply a very high form of practice and being so comfortable with discomfort that one can play in its presence and ultimately produce the highest-level results.

THE DISENGAGEMENT PRINCIPLE

In disengaging from performing and winning in these critical moments, leaders on the brink are following an ironic principle: The very thing we desire the most is what we must focus on the least. Climbing to the top of Kilimanjaro with only the summit as your focus—19,341 vertical feet and seven days away—will completely destroy your resolve in an instant. Similarly, focusing on performance and end game kill the ability to practice effectively in the moment and succeed.

Faith is the glue that connects practice to one's commitment, mission, and ultimate goal. Faith allows us to fully focus on the present moment and *trust* that the subject of our focus is essential to the execution of our overall goal. This seems counterintuitive, but think about when Michael Jordan took what has come to be known as "The Shot" in Game Five of the 1989 Eastern Conference Championship first round against the Cleveland Cavaliers. His team was down by one point, and there were three seconds left in the game. I assert that as he took the inbounds pass and released that ball at the foul line with no time left, he wasn't thinking about winning. He wasn't thinking about his mechanics, the trophy, how important this all was, or the diamond-encrusted championship ring he would get. He wasn't thinking about how he looked or whether he was performing well enough. He was thinking about the ball in his hands and the rim of the basket. He was thinking only about *hitting that shot.*

That's exactly why we're talking about him decades later, and why if you Google "the shot," you'll find countless hits. What I call "the disengagement principle" states that in order to be most effective and successful in times of high adversity and uncertainty, leaders must disengage from the egocentric attachment to performance and instead focus on playing the game in the moment, and *practicing* their craft. And yes, you guessed it: This takes *practice.*

HALF MEASURES

A "half measure" is something done with minimal effort so that it is only partially complete and not fully effective. We all take half measures to some extent in some areas of our lives. Leaders are aware of this and must not only limit the overall impact of half measures but also eliminate them completely from the places in which they lead. On the brink, half measures are not present. They undermine possibility and create the illusion of safety in compromise. It's similar to the impact of having a back-door escape route: if you know there is an easy way out, why remain committed when times get tough?

I want to separate this definitively from achieving perfection. The elimination of half measures does not imply perfection. Eliminating half measures is about raising our standards as leaders, declaring the level below which we will not play, and showing reverence for what we are trying to achieve through our leadership. Permission to practice creates the possibility of excellence, contributes to the ability to perform at high levels, and is essential to the fulfillment of big goals. Allowing half measures disempowers our resolve and lowers the bar to accept mediocrity.

Imagine for a moment that, going into that game against the Cavaliers, Michael Jordan had focused on the fact that the Chicago Bulls had been swept by the Cavaliers that season. The Bulls had lost all four games against the Cavaliers that year, and the odds were strongly against their somehow suddenly winning this pivotal game. These were conditions ripe for half measures on the part of Jordan and the Bulls; what chance did they really have anyway? A permissive attitude toward half measures would have eliminated the possibility of The Shot, because there would have been little impetus to even attempt it. Fortunately, leaders on the brink do not live in a world of half measures, because on the brink, half measures simply do not serve any purpose.

FULL MEASURES

All leaders whose names you recognize as a result of their successes got to that point because of the importance they placed on full measures. The *range* of a leader is expanded from their focus on full measures. Too often leaders pigeonhole themselves into one narrow area of effectiveness. On the brink, leadership requires a more dynamic and expansive view of what is possible. Each undertaking here comes from a place of full investment and unwavering engagement that leaves neither a back door to escape through nor any desire for one.

The question for leaders on the brink practicing full measures is not "Why would I?" but "Where else can I?" The context becomes one of looking for new places to lead, seeking additional challenges to take on, welcoming big ideas and big games to play, and consistently searching for what more they can do to grow. This question becomes their theme music for every entrance!

RESILIENCE

The brink requires resilience. Almost inevitably, all will not work out as planned. Resilience is born of a very personal combination of practice, faith, experience, reverence, commitment, and focus. Leaders on the brink cultivate this rich mixture for themselves so that it fortifies them and their resolve in moments of extreme adversity.

First responders are taught this through rigorous practice as part of their training. To become a Certified Wilderness First Responder, I was trained through simulations of situations in the most adverse of conditions: at night, alone, in the rain and cold, after being woken up from sleep, in several feet of snow, with few to no supplies available, and with people (sometimes simulated children) screaming for help. There were often multiple scenes to manage at once and varying dangers or obstacles present, such as a weapon's being wielded, an uncontrolled fire, wild animals, rising flood waters, steep slopes, and falling debris. To simulate the urgency of delivering care to victims quickly, we were on a time clock. We were thrown into these scenarios repeatedly in varying combinations and debriefed after each with immediate feedback and evaluation from our instructors and peers. The point was to build the experience bank for the unpredictability we would face so that it became completely normal and expected.

You can imagine that, at first, such an experience is stressful, overwhelming, and completely panic-ridden, with disastrous results. What occurs over the surprisingly short time of the immersive course, however, is that the shock of all those experiences very quickly diminishes and shifts toward normality. In fact, the training is specifically designed not to have you memorize what to *do* in every imaginable situation. It is instead designed to train you to *be* more effective and focused the more adverse and unpredictable the conditions. It is designed to have you practice normalizing even the most dangerous and catastrophic situations you could encounter, and to be able to practice the rescue-based knowledge you have accumulated in the presence of any set of horrific circumstances. That is resilience, and it is a practice.

This is what is required of leadership on the brink. Practice in adverse conditions so that resilience will be present during the darkest of moments. Leaders know those moments will come and prepare to be resilient in the face of them.

FORGIVENESS AND GRATITUDE

These may seem like strange subjects to address in the area of practice and leadership, but they could not be more relevant. The brink requires both forgiveness and gratitude at very high levels. As we have discussed at length, leadership is dynamic and challenging, inclusive of other leaders, and typically team based. Missteps, breakdowns, loss of enthusiasm, and diminishing enrollment will be present along the way. Milestones will be missed. Budgets will be blown. Systems will crash. People will quit. Someone will inadvertently hit "reply all." Leaders on the brink practice a healthy dose of forgiveness for all of it along the way. In order to powerfully move forward without dragging the weight of the past, judgments, complaints, and self-perceived "failures" along with you, forgiveness is the only solution.

We are typically better versed at forgiving others than ourselves, and to be leaders on the brink, forgiving ourselves is required for effectiveness and consistent forward movement. Forgiveness comes in many forms and through many different types of practices, including but not limited to deepening our spiritual connection, making daily affirmations, apologizing intentionally, and simply declaring ourselves forgiven out loud. However you choose to practice forgiveness, make it just that: a *practice*.

Similarly, gratitude is an essential component of leadership in that without it, we are simply striving for more, more, more, without ever taking inventory of all that we already have. This refers not only to material things that we have but also to our health, family, friends, joys, and freedoms. On the brink, gratitude sets a foundation on which to build what's next, because it assumes what we already have to be enough. From there, practice, innovation, and taking risks are no longer attempts to fill an existential hole. We are instead leading forward from commitment, passion, and intention. Like forgiveness, gratitude can be practiced in any way you choose, but the key is to make sure that the practice of it is consistent.

INTENTIONALITY

The word "intention" is used on the brink to mean "with specific purpose, and *on* purpose." Leaders on the brink take this type of purposeful action in the direction of their commitments. Intentionality is a fundamental practice of leaders, because it focuses energy, effectively leverages resources, and accelerates results. At the same time, it eliminates the possibility of superfluous actions and distractions that would otherwise derail both a team and its leadership. Intentionality as a practice simply involves *choosing* before taking action. Specifically, it involves choosing the answer to the question "What is this action serving?" and then answering it fully before actually taking the action itself.

On the brink, intentionality is the air that leaders breathe. It's all around them, and they are its source. They both practice it themselves and cause it in others. It's the not-so-secret secret to their success. It defines their actions and informs their cause at the highest level.

INSPIRATION

Most people wait to be inspired by their environment and circumstances before taking decisive action, which turns them into victims of circumstance. Inspiration has to find them, and all they can do is wait for it to happen to them. Or not.

You can see that this notion of inspiration does not serve a leadership paradigm. Inspiration is necessary, and it needs to be *owned*. Leaders on the brink own and generate inspiration at will and don't wait for it to happen to them. They generate it at every turn and create it in every endeavor and action.

The key to generating inspiration is to remember this fundamental principle: *Inspiration is purely invented. It does not exist intrinsically in any action or experience.* Think for a moment about the things that truly inspire you. They are not the same things that necessarily inspire others, even those close to you. In fact, they may not even have been inspiring for you in the past. The key is that they are each a choice. At some point you simply *selected* those things as inspiring to you. From that point on, that is how you have defined them, even if you've forgotten making the choice long ago.

Leaders on the brink remember that they are the source of what inspires them. As such, they can intentionally choose new things to be inspired by, or choose to be inspired by familiar things they once considered tedious or boring. In this way, *anything* is possible. Anything can become inspiring, and any action can be inspired.

TALENT

Talent in leadership is systematically overvalued. Such talent exists but not in the way we typically believe it does. This may be hard to swallow, but leadership is not simply the sum of your capabilities, knowledge, skill sets, and intelligence. It is so much more that it can, in fact, compensate for many deficiencies in those areas.

One of my favorite books on the subject is the aptly named *Talent Is Overrated* by George Colvin. Colvin talks about "deliberate practice" as the defining ingredient in the most talented among us. He goes on to detail that while challenging, uncomfortable, and often inconvenient, many times talent is precisely equal to the amount of practice put in. He uses Michael Jordan, Tiger Woods, and Mozart as examples of those who created their own superhuman expertise simply by *out-practicing* their contemporaries.

The greatest and most powerful leaders on the brink perform "deliberate practice" in order to develop their own talents and leadership, and also to foster talent and leadership around them. The power of practice cannot be overstated. It is the source of success, talent, and leadership and is available to every single one of us if we are willing to choose it and live with the consequences of that choice.

COMPLACENCY

One of the greatest dangers for leaders is becoming complacent about practice. Practice demands attention, energy, devotion, and nurturing. Leaders who forget this fact in service of getting "comfortable" are typically reminded rather unpleasantly about its necessity. Results dwindle, sales plummet, team discord develops, or dissatisfaction and disenrollment become widespread.

Practice is not optional. Leaders on the brink know this, and some have had to learn it the hard way for themselves. Practice is a daily necessity for leadership.

The best way to keep complacency at bay is to develop a relationship to practice similar to the one you have to brushing your teeth. You do it regardless of how busy, late, or tired you are. You do it when you don't feel like you need to, and you do it because you are committed to something greater than the convenience of skipping it in the moment. You don't just brush your teeth when they look dirty or if there's stuff sticking out from in between them. You brush them every day as a practice that has become expected and normalized. That's a solid relationship to practice that will inhibit complacency before it ever starts.

OPEN HEART

A conversation about leadership in practice would be incomplete without addressing the importance of leading with an open heart. Open-heartedness has been a trendy thing to discuss in recent years, but what does it really mean? I don't intend to assert what it means for everyone, as it's an extremely intimate and individually unique aspect of leadership. But generally open-heartedness is about remembering that no matter what type of leader you are, what industry you're in, or what technological component there may be to your goals as a leader, you are ultimately dealing with *other human beings.* This may seem basic and even obvious, but I promise you that it is one of the fundamental parts of leadership that is most often stepped over. Leaders on the brink must remember that where the rubber meets the road, they are not dealing just with numbers or profit centers but also with other human souls that possess their own highly personal needs, fears, joys, and wants.

Open-hearted leadership not only takes into account human needs and responses; it actually centers leadership *around* them. It includes the leaders' humanity as well as that of those with whom they work. It inspires leaders to listen on a deeper level not just to what their team and individual followers are saying, but also to what lies behind those words. It allows leaders to communicate transparently and be vulnerably open with their own processes in a way that is inclusive and inviting. It provides space for authentic communication and actually leverages the power of that communication as an asset to the team.

Acceptance of the importance of open-hearted leadership, along with the practice of and reverence for open-hearted leadership, makes the difference between good and great teams. It also separates the good leaders who get good results from the exceptional leaders who cause powerful teams to create impossible results regularly and effortlessly.

A great example of this is the Dalai Lama. He is a leader whose influence is born directly of his open heart, compassion, openness, and accessibility. Despite being in exile, he leads an entire nation strictly through non-violent ideology and methodology, even though the oppression by the Chinese government of his Tibetan homeland remains one of the greatest human rights violations in history. His commitment to open-hearted leadership in the face of such hateful behavior creates his following, even beyond his own countrymen. He is and has been a beloved leader around the globe for decades because of his leadership and teachings that come from such an uncommon place: his heart and his love for mankind, not just for his own people, and his struggle against their oppression. He inspires writers, political activists, spiritual people, and world leaders around the planet with how he chooses to lead from his heart consistently in the face of all the challenges he and his people face. Open-hearted leadership, like everything else on the brink, takes patience, trust, courage, and *practice*, all of which become most important when they are least convenient.

PRACTICE

CHAPTER SNAPSHOT

- Practice is distinct from performance.
    - o In the highest levels of performance, practice is actually present and prominent.
- The Six Principles of Practice
    1. *Persistence*
    2. *Intentionality*
    3. *Urgency*
    4. *Curiosity*
    5. *Commitment*
    6. *Play*
- On the brink, comfort is a trap, and discomfort is a practice.
    - o Here leaders look for places to practice being uncomfortable and normalize the presence of discomfort.
    - o They create an empowered relationship to both practice and discomfort.
- The disengagement principle states that leaders, when faced with adversity, are most effective when they disengage from focusing on the overall end result and instead focus on the next step toward that result.
- Talent is simply a function of practice and can be developed simply by applying practice to a developing skill set.
- Being an expert is a function of having practiced sufficiently to become adept at the level of expert.
    - o Malcom Gladwell states that the level of expert is achieved only after 10,000 hours of practice.
- Leaders on the brink are wary of complacency and adept at interrupting it before it slows progress.
    - o They do this by creating a habit of practice that does not allow for activity to become rote.
- Open-hearted leadership is a key to the brink in that it allows for intimate connection between the leader and the team.

    o   It creates relationship and allows for humanity, forgiveness, and gratitude.

EXERCISES/QUESTIONS

1. Make a list of the top three places you expect performance without practice.
   - Schedule regular (at least weekly) practice in each of those areas.
   - Make sure this practice is not judged or made wrong in any way. The only intention is to practice without the expectation of performing.

2. Make a list of the five areas of life in which you have become comfortable.
   - For each, identify three ways to make that area uncomfortable in a manner that specifically serves the result you are after.
   - Take on adding one of those ways to each area of life this week.
     - o Pick another for each of the five areas of life next week and add it.
     - o Do the same for the next three weeks.

3. Make a list of the three places in your life that you want to develop talent.
   - Choose how much time you are willing to devote to each area.
     - o Schedule that time in each area daily.
     - o Practice executing the schedule no matter how you feel in each moment.

4. For the next 24 hours, practice opening your heart as a leader in the times when you most want to close it and exert force or control.
   - See what difference it makes for you and for those you lead and lead with.

o Extend this time to the next 48 hours and then the next 72 hours.

◊ Notice the experience of vulnerability this requires.

◊ Practice being with that discomfort and moving into it rather than away from it.

"It's never crowded along the extra mile."
—Wayne Dyer

CHAPTER 5

COLLABORATE

THE POWER OF MORE THAN ONE

Collaboration is a partnership among group members that is specifically focused on a common intention or goal. The biggest, most challenging mountains are climbed by teams, not individuals. The bigger the mountain, the bigger the challenge and the more necessary the collaboration.

Leaders on the brink know this and build teams commensurate with the size of the mountain they have chosen to climb. In fact, they use the power of collaboration to enroll the team itself. Collaboration is attractive; people naturally want to be part of something greater than themselves, something in which their presence *matters*.

Collaboration is essential to the success of big endeavors; it exponentially increases effectiveness, scope, and possibility. Snafus—illness, frustration, resignation, lack of enthusiasm, the dreaded "reply all"—will inevitably happen along the way to any goal. While someone working alone might be sidelined by one of these events, a team of collaborators would be able to more effectively absorb the impact, bear the consequences, and keep the mission on track.

NOT ALL LEADERS NEED FOLLOWERS

Effective collaboration among team members generates the team. But it is important to remember that leaders of effective, collaborative teams do not just have followers in their ranks; they have more leaders. This does not imply "too many cooks in the kitchen" but rather a group of individuals each relating to themselves as leaders in their roles all focused on and enrolled in the vision and mission of the team.

The relationship between leader and team is unique and dynamic. All members of the team are expected to be leaders in the role they play, and in doing so, are constantly aware of their direct responsibility for the team's success. The team leader is responsible for relating to each member as a leader individually and at the same time holding the vision and mission for the entire team, owning its ultimate success.

There is no need for hierarchy or "rank" on a team with regard to the value of the individual members. This means that while there is a leader of the team, the relationship is not one of being "above" or "higher than" others. Collaboration implies a level playing field in that all team members are essential in their specific contribution. Leaders on the brink understand that the old model of hierarchy is outdated and limited; it stifles and controls rather than empowering and creating collaboration.

THREE COMPONENTS OF POWERFUL COLLABORATION

Three vital components create collaboration for the leader on the brink:

1. **Enrollment**—Effective and powerful collaboration requires enrollment and the ideological commitment of the entire team. Without sufficient and repeated enrollment, collaboration will be weak and ultimately ineffective. Leaders on the brink are intimately connected to their team and must constantly check on and reinforce their levels of enrollment.

2. **Empowerment**—Collaboration requires the empowerment of all the members of a team as leaders, allowing them to make choices that are in service of the mission. This level of empowerment creates ownership across the team at every level and a powerful, shared enthusiasm for the team's mission and vision. The effective collaboration of a team is directly proportional to its collective empowerment to lead at every level.

3. **Truth**—Collaboration at high levels requires unilateral, uncompromising honesty. At times the truth will be unpleasant to say and hear, but those are the moments when truth most serves collaborative team building. The team must subscribe to a high level of truthful communication, one that does not require filtering in order to protect feelings or status. This must happen before the mission starts, as well as during. When a team is engaged only with the truth, the ground becomes fertile for collaboration.

FOLLOW THE LEADER

Because of its treacherous nature, the brink necessitates followers; the magnitude of the endeavor intrinsically requires a leader to seek human resources to share in the risks and challenges to come. Yes, they will each be related to as leaders along the way, and they will also be following a leader as well.

The brink is *attractive*. Followers will *first* follow a leader and *then* agree to become enrolled in the vision that the leader embodies. This happens because leaders on the brink are intrinsically *enrollment worthy* by virtue of who they are. Think of the adventurers, visionaries, and pioneers of various fields. They create a following simply as a result of the leadership they embody by being willing to put everything at stake and operate boldly on the brink. Collaboration then becomes the byproduct of an empowered community of people curious about how they too can contribute to a leader's vision.

Leaders on the brink need to be aware, however, that this kind of enrollment in a leader alone is not sustainable. Followers ultimately want to commit to a vision that includes them and their own needs and desires.

Successful leaders on the brink need to demonstrate the savvy to present their followers with a vision big enough to include all of them intimately.

POWER

This one can be tricky. Take a moment to think of the five most powerful people on the planet. Now take a look at your list. Likely you came up with a list of recognizable names of famous people with a great amount of wealth, resources, influence, and control over others. This definition of power is outdated. In the paradigm of the brink, this old power structure is not only unnecessary but also ineffective.

All leaders on the brink are powerful in their own way, aware of both the source and consequence of their power. Power in leadership on the brink does not come from success, influence over others, or strength. Leaders on the brink generate their power from their leadership itself, specifically leading from love and heart.

This vision of power shifts the paradigm completely for most of us, and may even seem a bit "New Age." If you explore the idea, you'll begin to see the way in which this paradigm works to generate power. All that is required for access to power on the brink is the willingness to love one's vision, mission, team, and self unconditionally. Access to power is often misunderstood, but it truly is sourced from within. Leaders who are successful know this and leverage it to climb their mountains and lead their teams. This is why you *really* know the names of those five leaders; they exemplified heart and love in the form of a passionate commitment to their endeavors, and power was generated from there. While it is true that not all leaders are well known for generating their power from love and heart (Donald Trump, for example), the brink is a model of leadership that specifically relates to leading from heart as a more powerful source of power than the old paradigms of force, manipulation, and control.

Love, not force, inspired Martin Luther King's leadership in the face of consistent death threats. Gandhi chose nonviolence to respond to the British oppressors on his home soil. The Dalai Lama insisted that there be no retaliation after the massacres of Buddhist monks in Tibet. In each of these examples, the leaders' power came from their hearts, not their influence over others. That influence was, in fact, a *consequence* of the love and heart in each of them.

THE BRINK AS ACCESS TO POWER

Power is generated *from* the brink. This deserves a moment of reflection, because the implications are tremendous. Effectively, once we have found a mountain to climb, enrolled a team with which to climb it, and started on the journey, power is born out of the journey itself.

Energy accelerates along the way as adversity is encountered and overcome, new trails are blazed, leadership is discovered within, and a communal focus on the challenge ahead is formed. What this means is that we can count on the endeavor *itself* to generate power along the way, and that our biggest, most important step is the first one. From there, the brink conspires with us in generating and regenerating power along the way.

FIVE LAWS OF POWER ON THE BRINK

There are five distinct laws of generating power as a leader on the brink:

1. **Authenticity Is King**—Stop being careful, and say what you mean. Team members will respect this and expect it not only from their leader but also from one another and themselves. Power will come from that expectation and the trust that is generated.

2. **Team Is the Greatest Asset**—The most effective leaders are the ones with the most effective teams. Grow the team, and the power of each individual and that of the mission will grow with it.

3. **Have a Mirror**—Leaders seek other leaders, coaches, advisors, or masterminds for reflection and feedback in areas they may not be able to see on their own. Leaders on the brink know that the key to power is being aware of what we don't know, and finding ways to view what we cannot see.

4. **Get Needs Met Elsewhere**—The team is not an appropriate place to fulfill one's personal needs; this will absolutely zap the power out of the room. Needs to be loved, admired, liked, affirmed, or thought of in a particular way... All such desires should be left

at the front door. When individual needs fight for air time with leadership, the mission suffers. That being said, when the team members leave the room and are not engaged in climbing the mountain, all must shift their focus onto themselves and make sure their personal needs ultimately are met, so that they aren't distracted or depleted when they return to the team.

5. **Continued Reinvention**—No team or mountain is stagnant. The brink is naturally dynamic. Leaders must know this and remain in a constant state of reinvention—of themselves, the team, and the process. This does not mean that the goal, vision, or purpose will change. What will change may be the path to getting there, the tools used, the resources being tapped, and/or the strategies for success. The leader on the brink must be proactive about deviations from the expected rather than surprised by them.

THE "POWER BOX" ON THE BRINK

What I call the "power box" of leadership is in fact not a box at all. Leaders need places to focus their energy when generating power. The power box is a framework for this awareness, and it includes the following five tools:

1. **360-Degree Reflections**—Look everywhere for perspective and solutions, especially when most stuck. Make sure to look for insight from people and places that you typically don't—like objective third-party observers who have no idea how long and hard the process has been thus far. That's often exactly why they are so valuable.

2. **Outliers' Influence on the Center**—Remember to bring on team members who think and operate differently from everyone else. Use them! These will be key components to success, especially when everyone's got the same idea and has had the same idea for a while. There's no better way to doom a project than to stay with the familiar cast of characters who all share the same opinions and views.

3. **Knowing When "Boxes" Show Up**—Stay vigilant, because boxes (restrictions that appear as the result of paradigms) can kill innovation and ingenuity. Be sure to keep an eye on ruts, strict courses of action/direction, things that are done in a certain way just because that's how they've always been done, and any other indications of thinking too much "inside the box."

4. **Courage**—Remember that there will be fear. Leaders must be vulnerable enough to reach out for support or simply say, "I don't know." It takes courage to lead. The fear will be there, and the courage to take action in the face of it defines a powerful leader.

5. **Comfort with Discomfort**—This sounds like a misnomer, but leaders need to actually become comfortable with the discomfort of the continually shifting landscape that they will be experiencing. Everything is moving constantly, and that's actually a good thing. Leaders on the brink *want* that kind of instability, activity, and energy. It's much harder to escape inertia than it is to make it work for you and keep moving. Generating power requires acceptance of the discomfort that comes with change and uncertainty.

POWER AND THE OPEN HEART

As we briefly discussed earlier when we looked into power, on the brink, leaders derive their power primarily from open-heartedness, along with love for their great endeavor, the possibility of their vision, those on their team, and the challenge of the brink itself.

What do we mean when we say "open-hearted?" It's a trendy term often thrown around, but what does it really mean? Being open-hearted as a leader means making the choice to lead in every moment, not out of fear of the unknown but rather an intimate excitement over the potential of it. Open-hearted leadership exists only in full collaboration with the team. It means allowing for all possibilities and eliminating the concepts of "failure" or "wrong."

We've all had experience with this mindset, like during the first few days with a new puppy at home, when he can do no wrong (even while chewing the couch). Other examples include helping out another human being who can never return the favor and the 57th time you get back up on your snowboard after hours of bouncing off the ground just trying to stand. These are all examples of leading from an open heart, and all grant access to power greater than any title or influence. We all practice open-heartedness regularly, even though we are not always aware or intentional about it.

On the brink, leaders lead with this mindset on purpose. But why bother? Why choose to lead from love, when fear is so much easier, more accessible, and more recognizable? Because, for one, fear is limited in terms of the difference it can make and the depth to which it can make that difference. Love and an open heart have unlimited power. For another, leading from love feels better not only to the follower but also to you, the leader. Don't take my word for it; try it on for size yourself. The next time people on your team make a mistake and appear to expect an angry, punitive response, try empowering them, encouraging them, and partnering with them with an open heart instead. See for yourself; how well does it work, and how good does it feel?

The question I am asked most often about this is, "But *how* can both love and power coexist?" The funny answer is that true power *only* exists in the presence of love and open-heartedness. Any other form of power is inherently flawed and ultimately leaves suffering and limited results in its wake.

The old paradigm of power pitted open-heartedness and power squarely against one another. It rested heavily on a culture of fear and resource scarcity in order to generate work from teams of subordinate followers. Love and open-heartedness were seen as signs of weakness, and force was the only trusted indicator of strength. On the brink, however, this is the opposite of the truth and can be a leader's downfall if misunderstood.

POWER LEAKS

The truth is that all leaders have power leaks of some kind. Savvy leaders on the brink know this and take responsibility for it. This way, they can identify and stop those leaks.

Procrastination, antiquated systems, fear, and slow decision making are all examples of power leaks that impede leaders everywhere. Most are not even aware of the presence of a problem. On the brink, leaders must not only be aware but also be willing to act in order to stop a power leak. For most, this means a strategic partnership with coaches or external consultants who can help identify power leaks that the leaders cannot see on their own. Ultimately it also requires leaders to consistently look for their own power leaks so that they do not go unaddressed.

Why does this matter? Because these power leaks, no matter how small, can ultimately sink the whole ship. They undermine momentum and power, and like any ship with a leak, challenge the integrity of the entire vessel.

THE OTHER TRUTH

The harder-to-see truth is that we actually *get* something out of power leaks. As mentioned earlier, human beings never do anything repeatedly without some sort of payoff. Even if it may not ultimately be good for you or your business, you are in fact allowing power leaks to occur because of the payoff involved.

But what payoff could possibly be worth power leakage? Perhaps it is the comfort of keeping everything small and manageable, avoiding risk, making less effort, or justifying one's failures. The job of a leader on the brink is to break this pattern of behavior by addressing the source of one's habit of relinquishing power. Effective collaboration depends on interrupting power leaks so that constantly plugging those leaks does not become the focal point of the team and distract them from the true mission and vision.

COMMON POWER LEAKS

Leaders experience a few common power leaks most often and must be especially aware of them:

1. **Integrity Breakdowns in our Actions vs. Our Words**. Not doing what we said we would compromises our integrity and undermines our power by devaluing the impact of our word. It causes us to lose faith in our own commitment and ability to fulfill promises and face adversity, and it erodes trust in those around us.

2. **Putting Relationships on the Back Burner**. Not giving your primary relationships, whether personal or professional, the attention they deserve, while focusing only on results, will undermine power almost immediately. This is a surefire way to compromise your connection to the ultimate goal and rob everyone of energy. The negative effects that often occur without our awareness are what make disregarding relationships really dangerous.

3. **Unhealthy Relationship with Failure**. A game played simply to win easily and avoid failure will invariably strip power away from its participants. The focus becomes failure prevention rather than leadership and innovation. This leads to stagnation and, inevitably, a complete collapse. The most effective leaders fail often and without avoidance, anticipating mistakes as part of the process.

4. **Attachment to Outcome/Results**. Getting attached to the idea of winning can create the kind of problematic relationship with failure discussed above. What's even more complicated is that oftentimes, this kind of mindset also implies that our own value is attached to winning and/or getting results. This isn't good for us, and it creates pressure and stress where it is least tolerable.

5. **Waiting to Move Forward**. Hanging around and waiting for enough confidence to move forward only leads to more waiting. It also implies that we are victims of circumstance, needing the stars to align perfectly in order for us take action. This one of the most common afflictions affecting leaders and teams.

NONE OF US IS AS GREAT AS ALL OF US

Leaders on the brink know that there is no greater power source than the team itself. A team can generate power even when one or more members of the team are down and out. The effectiveness of leaders working on their own is subject to the ebb and flow of their individual capabilities and energy levels, all of which can be disrupted by something as simple as a cold or bad mood. A team is also effective because it *exponentially* increases power, innovation, and momentum as a result of group collaboration. Individuals united and committed to a common goal tend to create more energy and focus than the simple sum of their parts.

Building an effective team is an art and a science. As such, there are both specific, necessary ingredients and subtle nuances involved in creating a productive team and leading that team properly. In my experience on the brink, there are seven fundamental ingredients to a winning team.

FUNDAMENTALS OF A WINNING TEAM

1. **Ownership**—One individual must take responsibility for everything and step forward as the owner or leader of the team. Owners (or leaders) do not do everything themselves, but they take responsibility for ensuring that everything *gets* done.

2. **Relentless Persistence**—In the development of a team, relentless persistence is key. Team members must be willing to do what it takes, be uncomfortable, and stretch beyond where they have stretched before in service of a common goal. This is not easy to teach, so leaders must seek out individuals who possess this quality already on some basic level, and be sure that relentless persistence is a muscle that is regularly exercised.

3. **Remaining Present**—As we discussed earlier, team members must remain constantly aware of why they are together but must also be brought on board with clarity of purpose from the start. Many teams have been undone by bringing on members who initially lacked clarity about the vision toward which they would be working.

4. **Accountability in Multiple Directions**—This is absolutely key. Team members must remain open and expectant of feedback from all directions. They must also be willing to give feedback to everyone else, including the leader. The most effective collaboration requires transparency and a willingness to speak and listen, regardless of who is listening or talking.

5. **Leading from All Roles**—All members of the team must consider themselves leaders in their roles first and foremost. This is necessary for the ultimate success of the team. No members can

afford to relate to themselves as unnecessary, redundant, or "out of the loop."

6. **Communication Structures**—There must be specific and effective communication structures. All team members must be clear on with whom they need to communicate, and that all lines of communication are open. Leaders must not assume this knowledge on behalf of their team members. George Bernard Shaw said it best: "The single greatest problem with communication is the illusion that it is taking place."

7. **100% Buy-In**—One might think that the fact that teams need 100% buy-in goes without saying, but it too often goes unsaid and unheeded. Teams live and die by the commitment level of their members. As a team is assembled, the leader must be sure to be transparent about the challenges ahead, the scope of the mountain they will be climbing together, and the fact that much of the journey remains unknown. This will help members feel that they are necessary parts of an elite team. The team members must also be made to feel that they are tethered together as they climb the mountain, much like actual mountain climbers. This strategy keeps secure the commitment to reaching the finish line and prevents any individual team member from slipping off the actual or proverbial mountain.

LEADERSHIP COROLLARIES

In my experience, the more subtle nuances of effective team leadership can be summarized in five leadership corollaries:

1. **Leaders Don't Manage**—There is no fixed structure to the mission plan, and this provides the opportunity for any leader on the brink to innovate. The mission clearly defines the goal, but on the brink it also allows space for leaders to create their own path to getting there. Management of the process in the traditional sense is not needed here. Instead adaptation, responsiveness, and innovation are generated along the way.

2. **Leaders Are Master Collaborators**—Collaboration is an art that needs to be cultivated on the brink through practice. Effective collaboration is regarded as a central key to the success of the team, and it is treated with that level of importance.

3. **Leaders Listen and Speak from Altitude**—Leadership requires wide and varied perspective. Leaders consider *everything* related to the ultimate objective, including contexts, beliefs, relationships, and trajectory.

4. **Leaders Listen in to the Future**—This is essential. Leaders need to act in the present while at the same time anticipating how their actions or inactions will affect the future. At the same time, they also need to be able to speak about the present *from* the perspective of their intended future. For example, the head of a startup tech company could take on a large amount of venture capitalist debt today in order to bring together the most innovative minds in her field. This will create a calculated financial burden that will be addressed by the value and profitability that those new team members will create for the company over time. At the same time, she needs to be able to speak to the team about profitability and expense reduction today, from her understanding of how she intends for the company to grow responsibly over the long term.

5. **Leaders Call Others Forth**—The most effective leaders create leaders around them through modeling. The importance of this for the longevity and power of a team cannot be overstated.

COMMODITIES AND ASSETS

The common financial distinctions of commodities and assets can be used effectively in this model of leadership to describe leaders' relationship to their team members. "Commodities" are raw materials, resources we use when needed and perhaps toss away when we're done with them. They are interchangeable, expendable, and non-unique. An example might be the computer you put at your employee's desk, the truffles you add to your signature pasta sauce, or the time you spend bottling your vineyard's wine.

"Assets" are resources that are also investments. You put energy and time into assets so that they grow and mature, ultimately ending up as the foundation for the future. These are the parts of your business that you nurture and expend resources (*i.e.*, commodities) on in order to meet commitments and create legacy. An example of an asset would be the employee you hire to use the aforementioned computer, the chef you've collaborated with to create a signature sauce, or the vines that have grown for centuries in your vineyard.

A problem arises when we forget this distinction between commodities and assets and start to relate to assets as commodities. This can occur because of pressure to do so (such as budget cuts, economic slowdowns, or industry downturns) or simply taking assets for granted. We start to simply demand more of people rather than keeping them inspired. We rely on rules and policies rather than leadership, responsibility, and ownership. We blame people and look for problems rather than collaborate to create solutions. We start cutting corners instead of attending to our relationships as leaders and producing abundant, complete work.

Relating to assets as commodities typically results from fear in the face of an experience of scarcity. This mistake kills leadership, longevity, and scalability for any team, and is a surefire way *not* to achieve whatever goal the team is committed to. On the brink, leaders must know the difference between assets and commodities, and make sure to remember that both must be cultivated in their respective categories. One cannot exist without the other.

COLLABORATE

CHAPTER SNAPSHOT

- Build a team.
    - The most powerful leaders always create powerful teams around them.
- Leaders don't need followers, but leadership on the brink will create a following of individuals who relate to themselves as leaders in their own roles.
- Power is an essential tool for the leader in collaboration, but it is a tool that is generated *from* effective leadership, to be wielded from the heart, not from the old paradigm of influence and control.
- The Three Components of Powerful Collaboration
    1. Enrollment
    2. Empowerment
    3. Truth
- The Five Laws of Power on the Brink
    1. Authenticity Is King
    2. The Team Is Your Greatest Asset
    3. Have a Mirror
    4. Get Needs Met Elsewhere
    5. Continued Reinvention
- The "Power Box" on the Brink
    1. 360-Degree Reflection
    2. Outliers' Influence on the Center
    3. Knowing When Boxes Show Up
    4. Courage
    5. Comfort With Discomfort
- The Seven Foundational Ingredients to a Winning Team
    1. Ownership
    2. Relentless Persistence
    3. Remaining Present
    4. Accountability in All Directions

5. Leading From All Roles
6. Communication Structures
7. 100% Buy-In

EXERCISES/QUESTIONS

1. Where are your power leaks? Make a list.
2. Declare action you'll take on each in the next 30 days.
3. What is the payoff to leaking your power in each area?
4. What does it protect you from?
5. What is the cost?
6. Use the three laws of powerful collaboration in every collaboration over the next 30 days—Note what happens!
7. Practice the five laws of power with your own teams and notice the difference that it makes.
8. Practice looking at the power box as a tool to access resources when stuck.
9. Make a list of the assets and commodities in your team and mission. Notice where you are treating assets as commodities and start treating them as assets.

"The irony of commitment is that it's deeply liberating—in work, in play, in love. The act frees you from the tyranny of your internal critic, from the fear that likes to dress itself up and parade around like rational hesitation. To commit is to remove your head as the barrier to your life."
—Anne Morris

CHAPTER 6

TAKE OWNERSHIP

OVER HERE

Leadership and ownership are inextricably linked. One has never existed effectively without the other. Ownership in this case refers to "owning" a goal and taking responsibility for every step along the path to that goal, such that every part of it and its ultimate outcome *belong* to you. On the brink, ownership requires that leaders not only be fully aware of all moving parts of their endeavors but also 100% responsible for the mission's success or failure.

Leaders on the brink first look to themselves or "over here" when the need arises to take responsibility for a problem or challenge. This is important, as the extent to which we own a solution is proportional to the possibility of its success. The brink model positions the leader as the center of everything that happens on the journey up the mountain, and more importantly, the owner of the ultimate results.

Taking on ownership for the actions and results of an entire team may seem overwhelming and even impossible at first. But the reality is that it is both possible and essential to leadership on the brink. When a team, tethered by the same rope, ascends the most treacherous sections of a mountain, all climbers become intimately aware of their individual importance to the team. Ownership on the side of a mountain, as you can see from this example, becomes obvious and non-negotiable.

OWNERSHIP IS LEADERSHIP

This notion bears repeating and further exploration: Leaders do not just own their teams. They also create a culture of ownership within the team such that all team members become individual owners of both their specific roles *and* the overall goal of climbing the mountain. Think of your favorite sports team. It has a coach and team captain, as well as natural leaders throughout the team's members. The team that consistently wins is the one that instills a sense of ownership in every member. The quarterback and the place kicker each realize he is as responsible for the team's success as any other member of the team.

On the brink, leaders create a bond between team members that makes the team stronger than any one of its individual parts. Ownership is what allows them to do this. When a team shares a sense of passion born of their collective ownership, their members become invested in their common goal on a higher level. This leads to more effective communication, self-generated motivation, and connection among team members. But none of this can happen without leaders who first practice full ownership themselves and clearly define themselves as "The One."

THE ONE

The One is a simplified term for ownership. Typically, teams will loosely and unintentionally delegate leadership to several people, but the truth is that by diluting ownership, we dilute the power of the team, its vision, and its goal. Although on the brink it is necessary for all team members to relate to themselves as owners of the goal, having a single, primary leader who also positions him- or herself as The One creates necessary focus, clarity, and strength.

On the brink, there are typically six distinct qualities of The One:

1. Leads as a result of enrollment and value rather than force and imposition
2. Is responsible for the impact of his/her leadership on others and on the goal
3. Is always open to reflecting on his/her leadership and power leaks
4. Is both present in the moment and responsible for future results
5. Creates leaders around him/her and empowers them to lead in their own ways
6. Is open-hearted and able to make difficult decisions at the same time

Ultimately, being The One carries consequences—but it is a declaration made in service of the team, not ego or status.

FEROCITY

Ferocity is an important and necessary factor in the ownership and success of a team. As mentioned earlier, leadership is inherently polarizing. In fact, leaders create an unintentional hierarchy by simply taking ownership and labeling themselves as The One. Once leaders have established themselves as The One, team members begin to defer to them. From there they typically follow their leader's lead, wait for instruction and guidance, and generally begin to relate to the leader differently than they do one another. Savvy leaders are quick to dismantle this situation before it becomes part of the team's culture.

Leaders are responsible for ensuring that their teams are not blindly following but rather invested to the extent that they are also relating to themselves as owners. This collective ownership along the ascent fosters tenacity and a culture of ferocity on the team. It compels members to invest in something bigger than what they would be able to create as individuals. The sum of the team becomes greater than any of its parts, and this causes ferocity to become contagious among team members. This ferocity becomes a catalyst for success and momentum, generates energy, equips the entire team to better adapt to circumstances as they arise, and acts as a battery that recharges itself as the team faces the challenges of the climb.

CAUSATION

Leaders on the brink are aware that part of their responsibility is causing leadership in others. This involves fostering personal growth, growth of the team, and success. People join teams and follow leaders to gain access to something they cannot create on their own. No matter how altruistic the endeavor of the team, its individuals participate because they see something personally beneficial within it. This may be the opportunity to develop leadership or skills, to enhance a resume, or simply to belong to something greater than the sum of its parts. The job of leaders is to know what personally motivates their team members, and to make that happens along with their broader goals. A team can make anything happen when all of its members are getting what they need out of it. This is not to say members need to, or should, have their personal needs met by the team, but their specific reasons for becoming part of the team in the first place should certainly be addressed and included in their ongoing enrollment.

INNOVATION

Innovation is a natural result of ownership. When a team takes ownership of a goal, and a leader in turn takes ownership of that team, space is created for new, creative methods, paths, and ideas. Notice which companies you recognize as the top innovators in their fields. They all possess cultures of ownership that aided in their success. Apple, Google, Southwest Airlines, Zappos, and other pioneering organizations in various fields all started with visionaries whose missions, teams, innovation, products, results, sales, and fortunes all came as a *result* of their ownership of their visions.

Once ownership is established, and each team member's unique and essential role is clear, the team as a whole becomes more plugged in to its commitments and values. Choice, rather than heavy-handed obligation, tethers the team members to their shared goals and to one another. Everyone has something at stake, and everyone has the freedom to explore and create.

INFLUENCE

Ownership is the leader's biggest source of influence on a team. This is distinct from the typical way we think of influence—as a form of manipulation or leverage. Influence on the brink pertains to the difference a leader can make; ownership is the best way for a leader to do so. There are four points of influence on the brink, and they are all subsets of ownership that enable a leader to make a difference:

1. **Enrollment**—Leaders are constantly enrolling and re-enrolling teams in their vision and commitment.
2. **Commitment**—Staying present to the commitment of the team and following up with action are essential.
3. **Connection**— Consistently facing adversity together creates connection that needs to be fostered by the leader.
4. **Urgency** – Urgency, when created intentionally, is a powerful motivator for a team and a useful tool for the leader. Leaders on the brink need to be acutely aware of both the source and the consequence of their influence. It is not something that is used to coerce. Instead, influence provides insight into why others follow the leader's vision. Ideally, it aids in creating a connection between the leader, vision, and team and generates even more followers.

INTENTIONALITY

Being intentional about ownership is critical for leadership. Responding to circumstances out of our commitment to the vision of our team is essential for success. Too often leaders make decisions out of reactions to their or their team's fear. Being intentional is a requirement on the brink. A leader who is being intentional makes choices that serve the mission, vision, and team in the midst of circumstances that can be emotionally intense at times.

Without intentionality, leadership becomes subject to the variations of circumstance and the uneven surface of emotional reaction. On the brink, *what inspires* leaders' choices is almost more important than *what* they choose. The true power of any choice lies in its source. Choosing out of fear tends to generate more fear. Choosing from power and purpose tends to create more power and purpose.

URGENCY VS. EMERGENCY

This is one of my favorite distinctions, because it can make a significant and immediate difference on any team and is readily adaptable to any set of circumstances. It also provides the individual and team with readily accessible power. In my experience, there are four distinct stages of action, comprising what I call the "Urgency/Emergency Matrix," in service of any goal.

With almost any large endeavor (and many small ones as well), most of us wait until pressure builds before we start producing results. In fact, many people are self-proclaimed "pressure junkies," declaring that they actually *need* pressure in order to perform. On the brink, pressure is a power leak, not a tool for producing results. Pressure typically causes us to react out of avoidance instead of intentionality. More toxically, it requires a crisis in order to create pressure and forces us to work *against* the imminent possibility of failure instead of working *for* a result. It strips choice and options away from us, and we become unfortunate victims of our own goals. The Urgency/Emergency Matrix outlines the pattern that is typically followed in this pressure-filled habit, and ultimately gives us a way of distinguishing the pattern so that we can change it.

THE URGENCY/EMERGENCY MATRIX

Space—Typically we begin any endeavor with a plan that allows for sufficient space (time) for us to achieve the goal. This stage, the most comfortable, lasts until pressure starts to build.

Urgency—We then wait until all that space (time) has run out and the need for action becomes inherently urgent. We've all done this—gotten distracted, lazy, or busy with more current "emergencies" and strayed from the timeline of the plan. This stage usually lasts until our tolerance for pressure runs out and options start to get limited.

Emergency—This is where things get interesting. This is where we typically start to see some movement, because we're getting close to having no choice in the matter any longer, and fear of consequences starts to build. Here there is a real sense of power loss. The circumstances now own us rather than the other way around. In this stage we go into reaction mode, feeling the impact of having waited. Taking care of this problem now interrupts the *Space* stage of our other commitments and lasts until we start to feel that without action, we may not survive.

Have To—This is typically where we take the most action, when the choice or option of doing anything else has been fully removed. In this stage we see a triad of unnecessary activity, tunnel vision, and frenetic action. This is the stage that many people require in order to take action, simply *because* the choice has been removed for them. Unfortunately, the conditions of this stage are not powerful or intentional. This is the stage where leadership breaks down and panic ensues. When choice is absent, leadership cannot also be present. This is the part of a mountain ascent that can be deadly for climbers.

Here's what to notice about each stage:

Stage	Action Level	Choice Level	Power Level	For vs. Against
Space	Low	Highest	High	For
Urgency	High	High	Highest	For
Emergency	High	Low	Low	Against
Have to	Highest	None	None	Against

As you can see from the illustrated Matrix, the most powerful stage to be in is Urgency. On the brink, it is most effective to create urgency *on purpose* and *early on* in the Space stage so that it comes from intention ("For") rather than as a reaction ("Against"). When managing Urgency and Emergency from the brink, it is most effective to actually *own* Urgency, before Emergency owns us. This means literally finding ways to create urgency on purpose when we need it. A good example of this is a false deadline that you set, one that is earlier than necessary. Even pressure junkies can create urgency on purpose, in a responsible way that does not jeopardize the team or goal. In this way, there is still energy and urgency but no longer victimization by pressure or circumstance.

"THE FIERCE URGENCY OF NOW"

On April 4th, 1967, Martin Luther King, Jr. gave a speech at Riverside Church in New York City in which he spoke of "the fierce urgency of now" regarding our withdrawal of troops from Vietnam. This line has been used by many orators since, most famously by Barack Obama in his 2008 election campaign. However, another line in that speech is even more applicable to the topics of ownership and leadership we have been exploring. In the line that precedes the famous one above, King stated, "We are now faced with the fact that tomorrow is today." He was referencing the fact that, at the time, the country had been stagnating on choices and changes that it repeatedly claimed were going to be made "tomorrow."

On the brink, not taking ownership of the present moment has consequences. As Dr. King alluded, waiting for change is no longer an option, because today is yesterday's "tomorrow." Leadership demands that leaders own not only their choices but also the consequences of not making choices or waiting to make them. On the brink, hesitation is usually an indication of a lack of ownership. There is no going back; time and leadership move in only one direction: forward.

On the brink, there is no boredom or passivity permitted, any more than there is boredom or passivity while climbing the highest heights of any real mountain. It is inherently uncomfortable to climb great mountains, and similarly, the brink does not allow for complacency. The brink is the crossroads where adversity meets commitment, and this is where "the fierce urgency of now" is created. We can never assume that there will be a tomorrow. On the brink, we are regularly and intentionally confronted with the reality of what it takes to get what we want. The fierce urgency of now is an inextricable part of the brink and leaders who operate there.

DRAMA

Let's separate urgency from drama. What most pressure junkies *really* like about pressure is the associated drama that tags along with it. Drama makes things interesting if not effective. If you wait until things get dire and panicky, you'll likely win at the drama game but lose at the bigger game you are playing as a leader.

Leaders on the brink take responsibility before drama actually occurs, and they do this not just to avoid drama but because they understand the difference between urgency and panic: Urgency stems from proactively pursuing the result we do want, and panic stems from avoidance of the result we don't want. The most successful leaders know that this matters, because it affects the power of their vision and mission, as well as the morale, effectiveness, and longevity of the team.

The even bigger, more important difference is this: Urgency is an intentional *choice*. Panic is a fear-based *reaction*, and reactions by their very nature always happen too late to make any real difference.

Unfortunately, urgency is still something we often wait around for. As reflected in the Urgency/Emergency Matrix, we usually wait long enough for panic to remove choice and compel us to act. The pressure junkies who habitually mainline pressure do a disservice to their mission and vision, as well as their teams.

The aim of leaders on the brink is to fully own the part of themselves that is attracted to drama, interrupt it in time, and generate their own urgency rather than waiting to be driven by panic.

THE STATUS QUO

Leaders challenge the status quo by virtue of the level of ownership they take on. The status quo relies on familiar patterns. By definition, nothing new comes from repetition of the same patterns—certainly nothing worth climbing a mountain for.

On the brink, the status quo must be overcome and moved past. Innovation and creativity are paramount here. Leaders create a culture around achieving their goals and involve others in that culture. Purposeful urgency, willingness to abandon the status quo, and a willingness to serve as

The One are the trademarks of a truly successful leader on the brink who is effectively owning the team and its mission.

TAKE OWNERSHIP

CHAPTER SNAPSHOT

- On the brink, ownership equals leadership.
  - Ownership is akin to relating to yourself as The One—the person where the buck stops and ultimate responsibility lies.
- On the brink, there are typically six distinct behaviors of The One:
  1. Leads as a result of enrollment and value rather than force and imposition
  2. Is responsible for the impact of his/her leadership on others and on the goal
  3. Is always open to reflecting on his/her own leadership and power leaks
  4. Is both present in the moment and responsible for the f uture results
  5. Creates leaders around him/her and empowers them to lead in their own ways
  6. Is open-hearted and able to make difficult decisions at the same time
- There are four points of influence on the brink:
  1. *Enrollment*—Leaders are constantly enrolling and re-enrolling teams in their vision and commitment.
  2. *Commitment*—Staying present to the commitment of the team and following up with action are essential.
  3. *Connection*—Facing adversity together creates connection that needs to be fostered by the leader.
  4. *Urgency*—Urgency, when created intentionally, is a powerful motivator for a team and a useful tool for the leader.

- The Urgency/Emergency Matrix

Stage	Action Level	Choice Level	Power Level	For vs. Against
Space	Low	Highest	High	For
Urgency	High	High	Highest	For
Emergency	High	Low	Low	Against
Have to	Highest	None	None	Against

- o Urgency, when created intentionally, is the most powerful mentality to guide leaders on the brink.

EXERCISES/QUESTIONS

1. Make a list of the top three projects/goals you are leading but not owning.
   - Write a "manifesto" for each about what full ownership would look like for you.
     - o Practice implementing that manifesto over the next 30 days in each project.
2. Choose one of the three projects you identified and be clear with the team that you are The One.
   - Practice the six distinct qualities of being The One in that project with that team over the next 30 days.
     - o What difference do you notice that it makes for you to be The One there?
     - o Get feedback from the team about what difference this makes.
3. Choose another of the three projects you have identified and practice the four points of influence on the brink into your leadership there.
   - What difference do you notice this makes in your relationship to the team and their relationship to the goal?

4. Use the Urgency/Emergency Matrix to identify where you are on the Matrix in each of the three areas you have identified.
   - Write out what it would take to create urgency on purpose in each project.
     - o Practice creating urgency on purpose in each project over the next week.
     - o Be sure to enroll your team in it first!

"All power is a trust; we are all accountable
for its exercise; from the people and for the
people all springs, and all must exist."
—Benjamin Disraeli

CHAPTER 7

TRUST

TRUST AS FAITH

The brink requires trust in the form of faith—the fundamental belief that a goal is not only possible, but that you *will* achieve it, despite a lack of evidence for that. In fact, the brink often requires leaders to have faith in the face of evidence that often times *opposes* their goals! Consider winning NFL quarterbacks. The best of the best have short-term memories. They do not hang onto bad memories of the last play and pay little attention to odds. Their focus is on the *next* play, *this* game, all in the face of their opponents' intentions and odds that are often stacked against them.

POSSIBILITY VS. PROBABILITY

The brink requires a short memory too. The past is of no consequence there, and neither are evidence or odds. On the brink, leaders play a game of *possibility*, not *probability*. The likelihood of an outcome is of little consequence, because on the brink we are typically attempting what has never been attempted before. There are no odds to study, nor is there evidence to fall back on.

On the brink, faith is required; evidence is not. In fact, evidence actually gets *in the way*. Once evidence is found (if it is found), it can actually limit the innovation, vision, and attention of a team. Even the search for evidence is a distraction and power leak for the leader and the team, taking energy and resources away from the possibility of forging a path into the unknown.

As a result of our culture's voracious consumerism, constantly growing demand for innovation, and limitless access to information, leaders today must regularly confront the unknown. There is no longer an evidence-based foundation on which to rely; everything is being reinvented and updated continuously. In this environment, leadership requires a special type of faith. This type of faith is not born out of confidence or a track record of prior success—it comes purely from *choosing* to have faith. This faith is invested in oneself first, regardless of the outcome, and in the success of said outcome second.

On the brink, faith and trust are defined more as tools than things that must be earned. This is the same faith you exercise when becoming a parent for the first time. This faith is simply a decision to believe in a goal that you have never attempted. It's all uncharted, and it's all a choice.

TRUST IN PRACTICE

On the brink, trust manifests in many ways: trust in team, the vision and mission, ourselves, and the path unfolding before us. The practice of trust is done without judgment or prejudice. All trust on the brink stems from a foundational trust that leaders feel for themselves. Trust becomes the glue that holds the team together as it climbs the mountain, and its importance grows with the scale and scope of the challenges that the group faces as it climbs. This trust glue is essential, because it creates the possibility of overcoming obstacles and challenges as they arise with clarity, poise, and effectiveness.

Trust is self-generated on the brink. Because it empowers leaders to become the source of their own sense of trust, it is a powerful tool for leadership and success on the brink. It eliminates the problem of developing and depending on favorable external circumstances or evidence, which are unreliable and often nonexistent on the brink.

BURN YOUR BOATS

When Alexander the Great landed his army on the beaches of Persia in 348 B.C., he unloaded his troops and burned the boats on which they arrived. He then turned to his men and said, "We go home in Persian ships or we die." What Alexander the Great's proclamation served to do was limit and thereby manage options. He left no choice but to have faith in success, no available option outside of victory except for death. His army went on to win a battle in which it was largely outnumbered, its victory the result of the members' having no "alternative escape" during the fight. They literally had to win or die.

While you may not be facing such extreme situations, this example's context is central to the brink. We can intentionally generate faith in an outcome and ourselves by not allowing ourselves any other option. Unidirectional focus on a goal is fundamental to success as a leader on the brink. Commitment means leaving no back doors, excuses, or escape routes on the path toward your goal. It requires clarity of purpose, courage, urgency, and a willingness to trust in one's capability. That trust is solidified by figuratively burning your boats before climbing your mountain.

HOPE

At this point, it is valuable to distinguish faith from hope. Hope is a passive tool in that it most typically relies on the alignment of external circumstances. Faith, as we have seen, however, is an active choice that, while based in trust, also involves actions taken in service of our stated goal. Faith requires a participatory relationship with our results while trusting that they will come to fruition. To be faithful means to pursue our goals in a way that *informs and causes* our intentional action. Having faith in a team we are playing on causes us to stand strong in the face of adversity that would have otherwise stopped us.

THE "HOW TRAP"

One of the biggest roadblocks to leadership on the brink is the focus on *how* a particular mountain will be climbed *before* it is chosen. This focus is what causes most individuals, leaders, and teams to stop before they even get started; they make their choices of what goal to pursue contingent on knowing exactly how they'll achieve it. In what I call the "how trap," possibility is no longer meaningful. The trap forces us to be dependent on the probability and evidence of success before choosing to start. In the how trap, there is no room for chance or new discovery. Innovation is precluded.

Leaders on the brink have enough trust in themselves and their teams to take on climbing a mountain without seeing the path fully before getting started. Having to know how it will be done before starting interferes with trust by demanding evidence, favorable probability, and a proven plan for success right from the get-go. On the brink, though, the mountain comes first, and the "how" unfolds from there. The mechanisms that make this possible are faith and trust in our ability to do what it takes to succeed.

EXPECTATION

Buddhists teach that desire and expectation are the root of all suffering. They lead to a false sense of external need and, ultimately, disempowerment. Expectation is not "bad" or "good" but rather a common experience that we must remain aware of so that we can take responsibility for its consequences. On the brink, expectations can be dangerous. During a climb up the side of a mountain, expecting the weather to stay consistent, our anchors to hold, or someone to rescue us if we get in a bind can literally be deadly.

Leaders on the brink need to mitigate expectations by generating ownership of the goal in each team member. All the members must be fully aware of their roles in achieving the goal so that their execution of said roles is empowered and effective. In this way, expectations can be met, and when they are not, the reasons for this occurrence are owned and addressed immediately by the team. Leaders on the brink manage their expectations and *create* what they expect to happen. In this way, they actually generate trust itself as well.

RISK

The brink demands risk-taking. This is one of the many reasons that trust and faith are so essential. Leaders on the brink must have "skin in the game" and must call on their teams to do the same. Unless there is something at stake for everyone, team members will have different levels of investment and connection. This type of risk requires trust in more than just the probability of success; it requires trust in our own leadership and that of our team.

Inherent to taking a chance on the brink is the possibility of failure. The requisite willingness to put success on the line is part of what makes some teams win. Leadership becomes infinitely more potent when those who are being led have something at stake and are thus more deeply committed to obtaining results. This means that all members are putting something "on the line" by participating in the first place. What they are putting on the line may be money, reputation, time, hard work, physical risk, and/or time away from family.

RISK LOADING

Whatever leaders or team members choose to put at risk must be something they are fully invested in. As a coach, I know that in order for people to make a significant shift in their leadership, they must load the risk in the area that they want to shift. For example, if you want your company's profitability to go from scarce to abundant, you must put more money on the line, not less. Simply cutting expenses does not shift the culture that created the scarcity in the first place. That culture's context of scarcity will simply create more scarcity if we try to maneuver around the context. The only way to create lasting change in that experience is to change the culture and its context *in the presence of* the risk or expenses. If you load that risk on purpose, you can actually drive and cause the change in the culture.

You must first *experience* abundance before you can create it in your physical world. Abundance is not defined by a number of dollars in the bank but by the way in which you *relate* to those dollars. There are wealthy people who relate to themselves as poor, never having "enough," and poor people who are wealthy in ways that are not measureable.

The vast majority of lottery winners end up broke, or at least poorer than they were before they won. In an article from March 2011, *Smart Money Magazine* reported findings from a study conducted by economists from University of Kentucky, University of Pittsburgh, and Vanderbilt University. From a pool of over 35,000 lottery winners, they found 1% of them went bankrupt within five years of winning. That may not sound like a lot, but that number is over *twice* the rate of bankruptcy for the rest of the population. The winnings changed nothing with regard to the winners' financial sustainability or experience of wealth. They had not shifted that context, and so it ate through their winnings just as it had eaten through finances in their lives before they won.

Similarly, if you want to find more time, put more appointments on your calendar and gain the experience of conquering that challenge. Only in that way will the context of scarcity be shifted. Filling a bank account or clearing a schedule does not actually shift anything fundamentally.

You cannot make a significant change or surmount any big challenge without putting that thing at risk. Leaders on the brink do this on purpose by risk loading—creating increased investment or risk on purpose so that they are required to shift a context in order to produce the resulting change or movement they are after.

Faith allows for this change to occur, as there must first be a willingness to risk the things, beliefs, and habits that got us into the situation we are trying to exit. Throughout this process, faith in ourselves, our teams, and the possibility of a different experience allow for significant results to be realized. On the brink, risk and faith are inseparable. They work together as tools for leaders to use to move aside whatever obstacles may get in the way on the path to the summit.

GENERATING TRUST

People typically relate to trust as something that must be earned by the actions of individuals. This type of thinking inhibits leadership. Leaders without trust in their teams are like single jugglers on stage. They are limited by what they can manage on their own. Without trusting those around them, they must keep everything moving themselves and have no one to fall back on.

On the brink, leaders must be willing to implicitly trust those around them as leaders. They *give* their trust rather than forcing people to earn it. They must call others to leadership, foster their leadership, and relate to them as leaders along the way. Often this means putting great tasks and essential decisions in the hands of others and being willing to accept the consequences either way. This does not mean blindly giving something to people that they have not been trained to handle, but it does mean that once you train people and bring them onto the team, you give them trust and accountability.

This is why teams work. Responsibility and risk are shared and accompanied by trust. In this way, teams can do much more and climb much higher together than any of the individuals ever could on their own. The collective effectiveness of a team is greater than the sum of its parts. The trust members give and receive every step of the way plays an important role in the team's success.

The most effective leaders on the brink know that, in order to foster leadership in others, they must allow for failure. Failure creates an opportunity for true learning and ownership, plus the experience of the consequences of wielding responsibility. No one has ever learned to walk, ride a bike, or lead a team without having trusted, been trusted, and subsequently fallen at some point. Trust emboldens us to accept falling. Trust gives us the willingness to get back up after having fallen and has us practice and thereby strengthen that trust every time we fall and rise again. This new muscle increases speed and effectiveness, and strengthens the willingness to risk more and climb higher.

TRUST

CHAPTER SNAPSHOT

- The brink requires trust as faith not only that the goal is possible but that it will happen.
- Trust in this model is based in possibility, not in probability.
  - Possibility is unlimited and based in commitment and vision.
  - Probability is limited by the evidence of past experience. It is based on odds and measuring likely failure.
- Burning your boats is a way of closing off all escape routes and back doors to the successful achievement of the goal so as to focus your and your team's attention on winning.
  - It intentionally limits the options available so as to eliminate their distracting nature.
- The how trap outlines the fact that the question "How?" derails most goals before they are ever attempted, because the question is asked before the commitment and choice are made.
  - The answer to the question "How?" will unfold once the choice to move forward is made and the first steps taken.
  - The truth is that much of it will have to be discovered and is impossible to figure out beforehand.
- Risk loading is a tool of leaders on the brink. They intentionally create risk so as to overcome or shift an unwanted pattern.

EXERCISES/QUESTIONS

1. Make a list of the situations/areas in which you fully trust and truly know that you will succeed.
   - Practice adding one situation/area to that list weekly because you choose it, not because you have evidence to support that you will succeed in that situation.
2. Choose one area per week in which you will "burn your boats."
   - Practice sharing the intention with your team or partner and enrolling them in holding you accountable to implementing your intention.

- Notice the shift in the energy and momentum of the situations you choose.
3. Practice responsibly saying "Yes" to things without having to know "how."
   - Start small, in less impactful areas, and as you get more practiced at it, say "Yes" in areas where the stakes are higher.
4. Pick one area in which you will intentionally risk load (committing additional time, money, resources, etc.)
   - As you raise the heat under that proverbial frying pan, notice how much more quickly you are compelled to make changes, shift patterns, and move forward.

"In order to learn the most important lessons of life, one must each day surmount a fear."
—Ralph Waldo Emerson

CHAPTER 8

WELCOME FEAR AND ADVERSITY

FEAR, REVISITED

Most of us do whatever it takes to avoid what we fear, especially what we fear most. On the brink, leaders are required to constantly venture precisely in the direction of their fears, past the confines of their comfort zones. This is precisely why leaders on the brink use their fear as a guidepost, lighting the way to action, rather than avoiding it.

If leaders are not challenged by their fears regularly, they are likely playing too small a game. Fear is simply an indication that we are in the presence of or about to enter unfamiliar territory with uncertain outcomes. Many things we fear, such as death, losing all our investment, injury, etc., are realistic. Other fears, such as others' disapproval, looking silly in front of others, public disgrace, etc., are self-generated and made up, and these are the ones that stop leaders most often.

For leaders, fear is something to celebrate and move toward responsibly. An effective relationship to fear uses it as a *beacon* rather than something to avoid. The greatest leaders are not afraid of their fear but are curious and willing to move forward *with it* rather than waiting for it to subside or removing it. In this model, fear is a regular companion along the way—something to inform our planning—but not something that should ever stop us. For most, this model completely reinvents their relationship to and with their fear, and enables their success as a leader on the brink.

NORMALIZING OBSTACLES

The brink requires leaders to generate obstacles on purpose in order to give leadership something on which to exercise its muscles. The proverbial mountain a leader chooses to climb is one such obstacle. Obstacles are the fodder for our work as leaders. They are part of the program. Consider that if such mountains and obstacles were not present, leadership would not be necessary. What would there be to lead people through? They simply would not need leadership, the same way a small boat does not need a seasoned captain while tethered to shore on a calm lake.

The natural consequence of creating obstacles is that obstacles create fear. Human nature creates the tendency to avoid fear and obstacles; we are taught to do this almost continuously by parents, media, and especially experience and practice. As leaders on the brink, we need to be keenly aware of this and at the same time willing to generate our leadership in the face of this tendency and move through it.

On the brink, obstacles are both the source of our greatest opportunity and our greatest challenge as leaders. This is the fragile line we walk: we intentionally create that which will challenge us most and at the same time give us the best chance of success and growth.

In the military, the sound of bullets whizzing by your head becomes normal; it's part of the job. It's actually *dangerous* to relate to it as abnormal and to in any way be surprised or thrown off guard by it. Instead of reacting to the sound, recruits are trained in *intentional response*. This means they should identify the source/threat and ultimately neutralize it. We need to train ourselves similarly in business, in life, and on the brink: address the obstacle and the fear intentionally, while normalizing its presence. In fact, normalization is what actually allows for the effective response.

THE END OF NORMAL

The need to normalize fear begins where your expectations (what you already know to be "normal") end. Leaders normalize fear in order to respond rather than react. To begin normalizing at this level, we must simultaneously redefine normal.

When on a mission, what's easy, comfortable, familiar, or otherwise relied on as a crutch to make life easier must be set aside. We cannot rely on these things, because they rarely exist on the sides of mountains. They are also no longer necessary on the brink, in the same way that we no longer need training wheels and the comfort that they bring once we are able to race in a triathlon. The huge disparity between riding a bike with training wheels and racing in a triathlon is intended to highlight the extent to which ease, comfort, and familiarity are no longer needed. In fact, continuing to rely on these things and relate to them as normal is detrimental to leaders on the brink and creates a false sense of security. Circumstances may seem fixed and predictable when, in reality, they are very amenable to change. When leaders choose a mountain, build a team, and start the climb, everything previously defined as normal must be left behind.

Leaders on the brink must prepare for the end of normal by managing their expectations of how things will go and what will happen along the way. In leadership, specific obstacles cannot typically be foreseen, so anticipation can instead limit the possibility of effectively responding in the moment. The old adage "The only constant is change" is an absolute here, and this is what makes normalization a requirement on the brink.

VISIBILITY

Public speaking is the single most common response to the question "What scares you the most?" This is because one of the fears we are most affected by is being "seen" by others and thereby judged and assessed. This fear reflects our own negative judgments and assessments of ourselves that we project onto others. (We assume they feel the same about us as our most insecure selves do.) In fact, some of the fears we hold most deeply are the judgments we have of ourselves. Visibility creates the possibility that others will see us and have those judgments of us as well.

On the brink, leaders not only risk visibility—they expect it, seek it out, and welcome it. This is not from ego or selfish desire for recognition but out of known necessity. Teams need to see their leaders in action, in process, climbing, facing challenges, and persevering. Leaders don't need to be perfect or always win, but they do need to be seen playing the game and climbing the mountain alongside their teams.

It is impossible to be followed without being visible. Leaders on the brink embody the vision and mission of the team; they created the mountain and generated the team itself. Teams cannot effectively meet their leaders for the first time at the top or only hear from them periodically. There needs to be some tactile connection with the team at all times so that they can relate to and learn from the leaders' example and process. Leaders on the brink welcome the fear that comes along with visibility, because that fear is necessary. Fear in this case is actually an indication that they are doing their job!

TRANSPARENCY

Transparency goes hand in hand with visibility. The cultures of trust and visibility combine to create leadership that is transparent about the mission, path, and process. The old paradigms of "just following orders" or "need-to-know" management are limited in effectiveness and possibility, because they are based fundamentally on protection. Leaders on the brink put structures in place to create enrollment, feed trust, build team, inspire transparency in others, invite collaboration, and generate relationships.

Responsibly sharing ideas, realities, curious inquiries, and unknowns with your teammates and colleagues defines you as an authentic, powerful leader. This is contrary to the stereotypical image of the strong, unaffected leader who knows everything, shows no emotion, and is never scared. That model is a fallacy best suited for Hollywood. True leadership does not deny its humanity, fallibility, or need for collaboration and support; it operates in the face of all of that.

But transparency is not a one-way street either. In the most innovative and successful teams, groups, and organizations, 360-degree transparency is the best mode for communicating with one another. In this model, everyone is given permission to be transparent about his or her own process, as well as give feedback to others about their processes, even those ranking "above" in the organization. Transparency creates collaboration, interconnectedness, mutual trust, and an even playing field. The savviest leaders want to hear others' feedback and are fueled by the open level of communication that this type of transparency creates. They also are clear about the value of transparency by giving feedback and sharing information with their team. They know that it is in service of their mission and vision to do so.

DEVIANCE

The old management version of leadership worked very diligently to repress deviance from the ranks. By creating uniformity, this repression was thought to produce effectiveness and focus. But repression draws focus away from innovation and limits the benefits of multiple perspectives. Individuals in this old paradigm learn quickly that their best shot at longevity and ascension requires staying under the radar rather than sticking out. This has the desired effect of eliminating the work and effort it takes leaders to address people individually, but it also simultaneously kills creativity, transparency, trust, and collaboration.

On the brink, deviance is considered an asset. The greatest leaders know that they need dissenters, eclectics, and visionaries. Some of the greatest undertakings and discoveries in history were thought up and taken on by these so-called "outliers." The first-ever proposition that the world might not be flat dates back to ancient Greek philosophy from the 6th Century BC. But it remained no more than a theory until a deviant named Ferdinand Magellan had to courage to sail off into the horizon in 1521 and risk falling off the earth's edge. Thank goodness for deviance.

WALKING TIGER SAFARIS

In 1999, while traveling the world, I found myself in Royal Chitwah National Park in southern Nepal. I'd joined a fellow traveller on what the National Park called a "walking tiger safari." We intended to actually come across a Bengal tiger while on foot. You can probably imagine that this was not the smartest idea, but at the time, I was lured by the adventure of it. Our guide told us to prepare by wearing hiking boots and carrying backpacks filled with water bottles. Arriving at the meeting spot, the two of us found we were the only ones in the tour, and our guide was wearing running shoes and carrying a stick but no heavy backpack laden with supplies like ours.

I was more optimistic than realistic at the time and apparently a bit oblivious as well, so off we went. Thirty minutes into the walk, we happened upon a black sloth bear, and only then did our guide deliver safety instructions. It was at that moment that I finally realized the severity of our situation. Basically, our instructions, should we run into another bear or a tiger, were to *run in the opposite direction of our guide* while he tried to fend off our predator with his stick. What he then would need to do if things got bad (and this went without his saying so) was to outrun the two of *us*. It's a bit funny in hindsight but not so much so out there in the middle of nowhere.

You can probably gather that we didn't come across any tigers, and all went well, but the moment of choice is important to explore: We could have turned back. We could have *run* back if we really wanted to. But we both (crazy as it may sound) chose to go on anyway. While I wouldn't take that particular excursion again, there was possibility in that terrifying situation that would not have been present in the safe confines of the hotel. In the presence of that adventure/danger combination, we chose to continue, and we chose on purpose. We made this choice both in the *presence* of the fear and *because* of the fear. We chose in search of possibility—the chance not only to see one of the few Bengal tigers left on the planet but also to see, up close, our fear itself. It was as much an internal journey as it was a physical hike among the trees.

This is the path that leaders on the brink also choose (contextually, not literally). Typically the brink is generated by some great external challenge or adversity, but externality is not necessary. Circumstances do not create the brink—we do. Fear is an effective access point, as it typically points in the direction of our greatest challenges, the ones greater than we know we can achieve. While it may be typical and comfortable to walk in the shadow of the illusion of safety, playing it safe tends to get in the way of leaders.

The truth is that we put ourselves at risk daily—driving on highways; signing legal documents; riding busses, trains, and airplanes; scuba diving; eating sushi—and we do so with unconscious ease. The difference here is that we have normalized the risk inherent in these activities and eliminated our reaction to the risk involved so as to mitigate fear. We must normalize certain risks in order to avoid spending the entire day gripped with fear. It would be untenable to be terrified of crossing the street or getting in your car every day, so over time we *choose* to accept the risk. While the fear may not disappear, it is not stopping us from driving to work or enjoying our sushi. We have *chosen and accepted* both the fear and the risk.

Consider that the brink is even more powerful when this frame of mind becomes habit. Walking tiger safaris aren't necessary, but choosing to move toward the fears that typically stop you as a leader is. If you think back to the list of great leaders we discussed in Chapter 4, they were all creators of change who succeeded in making a difference by intentionally venturing onto the brink in the face of their fear. Their common denominators, if you look closely, are likely adversity and overcoming the fear that came along with that adversity.

ADVERSITY

In Super Bowl XLII, the New York Giants were heavy underdogs to the undefeated New England Patriots. The game is regarded as one of the biggest upsets in Super Bowl history. The Giants were up against what some were arguing was the greatest team to ever take the field. The Patriots were called "unbeatable" on national television, while the Giants were regarded as simply "in the way" of the Patriots' inevitable 19-0 season.

Against daunting odds, the Giants won that game 17-14 on a series of improbable plays with seconds left on the clock. It could be said that the Giants' ability to play at that high a level was in fact a *result* of the "impossibility" of their challenge and the adversity they faced that day. The height of their challenge compelled their incredible performance and improbable result.

On the brink, probability becomes irrelevant in creating success, and our greatest adversity often gives birth to our greatest possibility. The adversity involved in creating and climbing a proverbial mountain actually fosters leadership and leads to the "impossible" results we are after. Because of this, leaders on the brink think of adversity as an opportunity and a roadmap for results. They move toward fear, discomfort, and challenges, rather than away from them.

THE GREAT FAIL

Facing adversity and fear on a regular basis and with intention means that you will inevitably confront failure. This is normal on the brink. Leaders on the brink expect and anticipate failure. Stretching into the unknown is not linear or predictable. We can expect that, by definition, any endeavor into the unknown will include failure on some level. It's strange to know this, step into the unknown anyway, and stop along the way because of fear or resistance to failure. It would be similar to jumping off a diving board and panicking half way down that you might get wet. You *will*. The fear is fine, but panicking or—worse yet—turning back because of it, is unnecessary.

SUFFERING IS OPTIONAL

While in Nepal in 1999, I did a three-week trek through the Annapurna Range in Western Nepal near the city of Pokhara. The idea was to get to Annapurna Base Camp, which is the initial staging area for summiting teams. At 13,550 feet, this camp is not considered an unusually high climb, but access requires walking up and through several other passes, and the route is rugged. Our trip was delayed due to an illness in my guide's family, so he and I ended up leaving just before the rainy season started. He warned me that there would be serious obstacles to face, such as the possibility of flash flooding and an absolutely certain encounter with leeches. I agreed to go anyway.

It started raining two weeks into the trip, during our descent. Flash flooding and leeches were ever-present. Once confronted with flash floods, I ran (as instructed) for higher ground. Covered in leeches, I panicked. Our lives were at risk every step of the way, and comfort was literally an impossibility. Each day, three times per day, we had to stop and burn *hundreds* of leeches off each other with cigarette lighters. His response to my initial disturbance with the procedure was to smile. When I asked why he was smiling, he simply said, "I smile at your suffering from the things you chose." That smile will stick with me forever.

Leeches and flash floods were great lessons for me on the way down that mountain, and my guide was a wise teacher. I had chosen this journey and *all* that came along with it, and then had *chosen to suffer* when those things occurred. In hindsight, I can see the humor in it. I can also see the learning opportunity of it all. Our choices come with consequences, and those consequences (whether we knew about them upfront or not) are *also* choices we must own. Even consequences we don't like are still ones we fundamentally chose for ourselves, and failing to understand this is what stops many of us when things don't go our way. But the truth is that suffering is always optional. It's especially obvious that it's optional when what we are suffering from is the direct consequence of our own choice.

Leaders on the brink choose *all* aspects of their journey; none of it happens *to* them. They also recognize that suffering is always optional and not always a bad thing. This concept is not new. The Catholic perspective on this is that one can achieve redemption through suffering. Lebanese-American poet Kahlil Gibran wrote, "Out of suffering have emerged the strongest souls; the most massive characters are seared with scars." We can learn a great deal about ourselves from our own suffering. On the brink, suffering is a choice and not always something to be avoided.

CLOSETS

Fear creates what I call "closets" for leadership. Think about the stereotypical closet, packed full of stuff that you don't want to deal with getting rid of today, stuff you have never (or rarely) used and probably never will, a place to hide the things you are afraid to let go of. Closets aren't just for skeletons. We put all kinds of stuff in the back corners and top shelves of our proverbial closets that we don't want to have to face: feelings, financial matters, relationships, business decisions, opportunities missed ...

Consider IBM executives' reasoning for staying out of the development of the personal computer in the early 70s: They believed there would never be sufficient demand for a computer in every home. Only large corporations or the very rich would buy such a product … or so they thought. After all, that's the way things seemed to be going. Why bother looking around in *that* part of the closet? Whoops.

IBM survived the "industry closet" in which it hid, but as a result, it lost the opportunity to be the leading competitor in the PC market. Whereas IBM used to be the number one name in the world of computers, it has not fully recovered and may never regain that top spot. Like the ostrich with its head in the sand, hiding from reality, people pay a consequence for closets. Fears and other things we are averse to looking at and being responsible for can become hidden, as can the potential rewards, if ignored long enough. On the brink, leaders are not only aware of the things they avoid by putting them in closets, but they also force themselves to constantly look inside said closets, pull things out, dust them off, and address them fully. Leaders on the brink have closets, but they are open and emptied often.

SABOTAGE

Many leaders sabotage themselves and their goals by filling their closets or pretending they don't exist. In fact, one of the greatest forms of sabotage is to develop defenses to protect ourselves from our fears and then pretend that neither the fears nor the defenses exist. This is how closets begin to overflow.

What is especially challenging about sabotage is that you will initially feel more comfortable, easy, safe, and familiar than you did without the sabotage. Its painless nature will lull you to sleep. Because it *feels* good, it is especially difficult to identify and interrupt. But as anyone who has failed to change the oil in his or her car for long enough knows, ignoring closets because we're comfortable will eventually leave us stranded by the side of the road.

On the brink, we relate to fear, protection, avoidance, and closets as part of our ascent of our mountain. We normalize and address each on a regular basis, looking for places we have a habit of avoiding or protecting. This is a *practice*, because it is continuous and never ending. Leaders on the brink know that their leadership, team, mission, vision, and mountain all depend on it.

SUCCESS IS OPTIONAL

On the brink, we say success is optional because it truly results from choice and is itself a choice. It results from the choice to move toward our fears and discomfort (which will surely be there at some point along the way) in service of our growth, rather than the choice to avoid challenges and adversity in service of our sense of safety and security. Fear is a natural complement to success, and while simply provoking our fears does not guarantee success, avoiding them virtually guarantees playing small and stagnating growth. The choice to be successful inherently comes hand in hand with the choice to face our fears and empty our closets.

Many choose leadership initially only to find that they cannot or will not make this fundamental choice. They repeatedly run into reasons not to move forward. Everything is too hard for them. They are victimized by overwhelm, and the goal seems simply impossible.

The choice of success is as essential as it is intimate. It requires us to acknowledge our feelings, doubts, fears, and discomforts, and to then do the most unnatural thing in the world: move toward them. The capacity to make such a choice exists in everyone. It is a terrible disservice to one's own potential to sit back and claim that leadership is somehow gifted to some and not others. All "heroes" and leaders throughout history have at some point made the *choice* to be successful, and have repeatedly done so in the face of their own fears, doubts, adversity, and humanity.

On the brink, the act of moving toward fear and discomfort must be practiced regularly. This allows access to the brink itself. All leaders must at some point face their own natural resistance, accept it, and then choose to move beyond it. This choice is available to each of us.

DRAMA, REVISITED

We discussed drama earlier in the context of ownership, and it is closely tied to our fears as well. Drama is simply an external expression of our fears, an indicator that fear is present. There is very little drama for leaders on the brink. They do not create space for it; thus it has no place in which to grow.

By initially and frequently addressing their relationship to fear, leaders on the brink interrupt drama before it has a chance to interfere with their mission. The absence of drama in the face of challenges or emergencies denotes a high level of awareness of this relationship. On the brink, there is only space to respond with intention and action, not to react out of fear in dramatic fashion.

Inherent in disrupting drama is normalizing the impact of our circumstances and the fear they inspire, thus eliminating the need for complaints. Otherwise, drama from this place is like buying a convertible and complaining that your hair gets messed up when you drive it. First of all, that consequence should be expected if you take the top down. Moreover, messed-up hair is irrelevant, given the depth of one's commitment to the experience of owning the convertible or the mission at hand.

THE PATH OF LESS CONVENIENCE

The brink is, by definition, "a path of less convenience." It requires us to prioritize possibility over evidence, commitment over feelings, mission over circumstances, action over comfort. There is little conversation about convenience on the brink, yet it is important to note that even with the brink's inconvenience, this path is more focused and intentional than the alternative. Because we are less focused on ease, we are able to put more energy into the mission at hand.

Inconvenience can be a great source of fear for people. Just take a look at the behavior of passengers waiting for a delayed flight; the reactions of people standing in a long, slow-moving line; or the frustration that can turn bad traffic into road rage. We are addicted to convenience, and when our next fix is threatened, we become terrified—and that fear often turns to anger. It's easy to see why so few people take on leadership endeavors on the brink; the addiction to convenience derails many before they start.

Leadership itself is a path of less convenience. It requires relentless exploration of the places we least want to explore and a willingness to do what it takes when we least feel like it. This is what makes leadership so rare. It's also the reason that leaders often default to managing. It's easier and much more convenient to apply pressure to a fixed system than it is to create, innovate, and lead.

THE CONFLICTING COMMITMENT MODEL

A common source of fear and distraction for leaders is the burden of taking on multiple obligations at once. Often, the many things we are simultaneously committed to vie for our time, energy, and other resources. Leaders must be aware of this phenomenon, both for themselves and their teams. Individual team members will often find conflict among their own chosen commitments as well as conflict between their commitments and those of the team.

This experience of conflict is invented and a form of sabotage. Enrollment and focus need to be used to interrupt the seed of conflicting commitments before it grows. This conflict will feel like the truth to those in the throes of it, but leaders on the brink are charged with holding the line. They must stand in the face of the conflict created between commitments and at the same time be in service to each commitment. This will enable them to re-enroll others to remain committed to their mission. The truth is that each commitment actually feeds the others, and the essential key is to be responsible for creating and maintaining them that way.

This is the principle on which many performance-based compensation structures are based. Employees are compensated based on how effectively they produce for the team and the company. Their investment in growing their own compensation thereby serves the team and company. By also serving the longevity of the organization, this in turn serves the employee as well. Company meetings, business trips, sales trainings, and client sales calls all serve the interests of each party involved, even though at times those different components may occur in opposition on a calendar and vie for the employee's time. This is not a "problem" to fix, but rather a symbiotic relationship to recognize and respect.

We must remember that, in the conflicting commitment model, conflict itself is nothing more than a story of our own creation. We must take our commitments and shift their context from conflict to *alignment*. The truth is that all commitments leaders take on are in some way contained within a greater commitment that is closely aligned with their vision. All the commitments inside that broader commitment *cannot possibly* be in true conflict unless we create them—conceive of them—that way. They are inherently integrated into the leaders' being and actions. On the brink, the *experience* of conflicting commitments is addressed early and completely before it actually has any impact.

UNREASONABLE

Being "reasonable" ultimately means being cautious and predictable. This is the opposite of what is required for leadership on the brink. On the brink, being reasonable is a liability. Leaders need to be in the habit of thinking unreasonably, as the mountain they have chosen to climb is itself typically unreasonable.

Looking at things through an unreasonable lens means not just looking outside the box. It also requires conceiving of the box as a completely fictional entity. This allows for unlimited possibility where leaders can enact *whatever they say* is next.

We are not used to thinking this way. We are accustomed to rules, parameters, SWOT analysis, risk management reports, and reconnaissance. But on the brink, we are almost always in uncharted territory. There is no "reasonable" way to navigate what has not been mapped. Unreasonableness in thought and practice must be a constant along the way.

Fear presents itself along the unreasonable path, and a leader on the brink both expects and welcomes this. Fear combined with unreasonableness creates a bold and heightened awareness. Leadership is an inherently imbalanced system of boldness and awareness that thrives on action rather than balance.

THE EVIDENCE MYTH

Requiring evidence before taking action is a self-imposed trap. By definition, if we need evidence in order to produce a result, then we can only ever reproduce past results. Yet there's comfort in evidence, proof, and a well-trodden path. It's the reason so many of us check references, invest in track records, hire people with diplomas, kick the tires, and pause action in order to "think about it." Evidence preempts and allays fear. Sometimes gathering it is the smart thing to do; other times it's simply a mask for fear.

In the area of innovation, evidence can actually be a brick wall. It can lead to inaction or retreading a path conveniently paved by someone else. There is no possibility of creating something new when we require evidence of its having been done before. Have you ever seen a corporation make a big change? It often takes *years*, if it happens at all. And this lag time leaves the company behind the curve.

Think again about IBM's reasoning for staying out of the development of the personal computer for home use. The company instead continued building and perfecting what was already out there, based on the collected evidence of the past, falling well behind the rest of the market before realizing its mistake. Now think of JFK's speaking before a special joint session of Congress on May 25, 1961 and *declaring* that we would send an American safely to the Moon before the end of the decade. JFK made this declaration knowing that he did not have all the answers himself and that he could not do it alone, but that it absolutely would be done. He had no evidence, research, or scientific proof of its even being possible at that point, so it was a completely unreasonable mission. Nonetheless, we put a man on the Moon on July 20, 1969, and likewise, there's a very good chance you're reading this on your home PC, laptop, or cell phone.

Leaders on the brink must retrain themselves and their teams to stop looking for evidence. If you're up to anything in any way innovative, then by definition there will be no evidence for you of what lies ahead.

EXCUSE PROOF

The need for evidence is the primary source of excuses. If you analyze excuses you have used in the past to avoid taking a risk, you will likely find they are based on a piece of evidence you collected some place along the way and held onto: evidence of things' not working out, of how hard this thing was the last time, of how "bad" you are at something, of how long it took others to complete, of the waste of time it was trying this before, of the countless people who have told you that it wouldn't work this time either, or some other general evidence of your failures up to this point.

Either way, evidence supports the excuses on which our fear relies. It has us negotiate with our fears, make concessions to keep them at bay, or put things off until the fear goes away. The truth is that you cannot successfully negotiate with your fears. They will just keep coming back for more once you start giving in to them.

The end of evidence means the end of excuses, as we are then left with the opportunity of nothing but the present moment and what lies ahead. Leaders on the brink know that the end of evidence will actually excuse-proof their endeavors, so they look for ways to remove evidence and the need for it from their teams and declarations.

THE PERSISTENCE PRINCIPLE

As discussed earlier, when faced with fear, leaders on the brink tend to lean forward rather than away. This gives them the power to move through the fear, keeping the team on course toward the goal, like an airplane navigating through turbulence. To do this, a leader must be persistent in the face of great fear and adversity.

The "persistence principle" states that the degree to which leaders persist in an endeavor is inversely related to the depth and duration of fear that they will have to endure. In other words, persistence keeps leaders focused on the future, not on present or past difficult circumstances. This effectively diminishes focus on the fear, as it leaves little time, space, or energy for focusing on how scary it all is.

Think about going for a long run. You persistently focus on the next step, the next mile, the finish line, etc. And as any serious runner knows, as soon as you start to think about your legs' burning or your lungs' filling with fire, everything crashes. Runners don't actually "hit a wall," as the saying goes; what actually happens is that they lose focus. That distraction *feels* like a wall. Persistent focus on taking the next step, and the next step, over and over again, relentlessly brings runners back into focus on the race they have ahead of them.

This is the heart of the persistence principle: Persistence mitigates the effects of fear in an individual or team. Persistent action can refocus our attention on moving forward rather than dwelling on how hard everything is and has been.

BEING WILLING WITHOUT WANTING TO

This concept falls into the category of "simple but not easy." On the side of any mountain, no matter how powerful or focused the team or leaders, a moment will inevitably arise when they will simply not want to go forward any more. It is in that moment that they will need to be willing to take the next step without needing to want to.

It is both unavoidable and necessary for leaders on the brink to find the power to move forward without wanting to do so whatsoever. Most people stop at the point where they do not "feel like" continuing. Leadership on the brink, however, is generated from commitment and intention, rather than temporary, shifting moods. Being willing without wanting to is best thought of as a muscle that needs to be exercised. This is why it's simple but not easy—the idea of it is easy to understand and align with, but the practice of it is rigorous, uncomfortable, and demanding. It requires choosing to do the thing you least want to in that moment, in service of your commitment. This is a cornerstone of leadership on the brink and part of the climb that will be remembered as being key to your success.

PROBLEMS

Managers have problems; leaders have challenges to take on. Defining a challenge as a problem is simply symptomatic of a weak reaction to fear. On the brink, when fear is expected and normalized, challenges do not seem like problems any longer.

Typical "problem solving" does more damage than good. It implies that something is "wrong" in the first place and creates a "fix it" mentality, rather than an innovative one. Fear that there's something wrong in fact *causes* problems. The problem solver regularly needs problems to solve and therefore tends to create them where they don't exist.

Politics is a prime example of this phenomenon. Political figures make decisions typically in reaction to a problem that they see or that is brought to them to "fix." Their solution is typically one that costs in ways that they had not anticipated, and that ends up causing additional problems. Look no further than the so-called "Bridge to Nowhere" project in Ketchikan, Alaska that has become a symbol of politicians' ineffective "problem solving" so much that "bridge to nowhere" has become a catch phrase to imply a poor solution to a problem that did not exist in the first place.

As the saying goes, when you use a hammer everywhere, everything starts to look like a nail. On the other hand, taking on *challenges* rather than problems is empowering and builds others' confidence in you. A challenge is an opportunity and is expected. Facing a challenge calls on your and others' greatness, while problems tend to diminish resolve and momentum.

THE LEADERSHIP MATRIX

Leaders on the brink focus on the future over the past. They intentionally take risks and innovate along the way. Managers, on the other hand, tend to rely on creating sustainable survivability. That's a fancy way of saying that they get comfortable with just getting by.

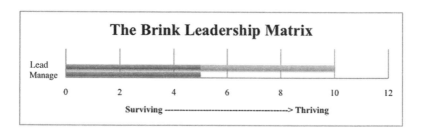

On the brink, leaders cannot thrive while they are focused on surviving. When one is thriving, on the other hand, survival is a natural outcome. Thriving is not fear based, while just focusing on surviving breeds and feeds on fear. Fear-based management creates a culture of survival that relies on the constant threat of some consequence or punishment. When climbing the mountain, a fear-based attitude focused solely on surviving the climb is not sustainable. It encourages separatism and erodes teams. A fear-based attitude is dangerous on the brink, because it focuses everyone (including the leader) on self-protection and avoiding disaster, rather than on the goal. This is the power-sapping downfall of many teams—focus is on anticipating negative consequences rather than on achieving success as a team.

Thriving requires focus and actually includes surviving, in the same way that being successful at work each day includes not crashing your car into a tree during your morning commute. Survival is an assumed ingredient in thriving. Unless your day includes a physically hazardous activity like climbing a mountain, survival does not require or deserve the attention and energy of planning your day around it.

STORIES

The fear we experience as leaders is generated by the stories we carry around with us and retell ourselves over and over again. Most of those stories are negative and limit us to small dreams. All of them are invented and based on the past.

Let's talk about the boogeyman. He's only ever as real as you let him be. But you didn't know that as a kid, did you? In your childhood bedroom, just as the lights went out, every small creak in the house seemed to be proof that the boogeyman was on his way to get you.

Do you remember what your parents did to chase him away? They turned on the light, inspected every corner of your closet, and shined the flashlight under the bed. They illuminated the truth behind the story for you. Well, the boogeyman is still around in each of our lives—he's just changed his approach ...

Now he can be found in the daily fear and discomfort that challenge or stop you over and over again. As adults and leaders, our new boogeyman is the conviction that we can't, that it won't work, that we're not good enough, that we're not worth it, that what we're up against is too big. And it's all still just a story. Only now the closet that needs searching is your commitment, the bed that needs overturning is your connection to your goals, and the light that needs turning on is the courage to venture onto the brink. The boogeyman, like all other stories about your fears, is of your own creation.

Leaders on the brink take artistic license with these stories. They tell tales of greatness and adversity overcome, not ones of easy paths or small pursuits. The stories they tell reflect their choices and resulting experiences. So, when you're on the side of your mountain telling yourself a scary story, remember to turn that proverbial light on. If you're going to go around making up stories, you might as well make them empowering ones.

WELCOME FEAR AND ADVERSITY

CHAPTER SNAPSHOT

- On the brink, fear is normalized and accepted, rather than mitigated and avoided.
  - o The entire relationship to fear needs to be reinvented for a leader to be able to take action in its presence, rather than waiting for it to go away.
  - o Leaders on the brink are willing to be transparent and visible with our teams, to face obstacles and adversity, to even risk failing, and accept the fear of each.
  - o Leaders here choose to actually seek out our fear and get curious about it so as to gain facility with it and learn from it.
  - o Fear is unavoidable, but suffering as a result of that fear is optional.
- Deviants or outliers are assets on the brink, because they provide alternate perspectives and contributions.
  - o The old model of requiring uniformity is ineffective at this level of leadership.
- Closets for leaders are places where we hide opportunities and unfulfilled goals because of our fear.
  - o Leaders must know that we have a closet like this, be aware of what's in it, and clean it out regularly.
  - o The best way to sabotage leadership is to ignore that we have a closet at all.
- On the brink, success is a choice, drama is eliminated, and inconvenience is normalized.
  - o Success is optional on the brink and needs to be a conscious choice.
    - ◊ The choice helps generate the success.
  - o Drama results from a weak relationship to fear.
    - ◊ Leaders on the brink create this relationship on purpose so that drama has no place to grow.

- o Convenience requires avoiding obstacles and eliminating adversity.
  - ◊ Neither avoiding obstacles nor eliminating adversity is possible on the brink, and leaders set out knowing this from the start.
- The conflicting commitments model states that no commitments a leader chooses are inherently in opposition to each other.
  - o They can be created that way unintentionally, but leaders on the brink integrate our commitments so that they source each other.
- Leaders on the brink need to be perpetually unreasonable in both our thinking and actions.
- The evidence myth highlights the fact that by definition there will be no evidence of past success when we are up to creating something that has never been created before.
  - o On the brink, leaders do not look for evidence; we look instead for possibilities.
- The persistence principle states that the degree to which leaders are persistent in an endeavor is inversely related to the depth and duration of fear that we will endure.
  - o Persistent focus and relentless action leave no room for focus on and distraction by fear.
- "Being willing without wanting to" allows leaders on the brink to take action from our commitments without having to first navigate our feelings in any given moment.
  - o This allows leaders to take action without *needing* to feel like it.
- On the brink, leaders have challenges to face, not problems to overcome.
  - o Challenges are exciting to face, while problems are exhausting to have to fix.
- The Leadership Matrix shows that leaders focus on thriving rather than surviving.

- o Surviving is inherently included in thriving and rarely warrants focus.
  - ◊ On its own, surviving just creates protection from and focus on failure.
- We all tell ourselves stories in our heads and in our contexts and fears.
  - o The key is that our stories are all invented.
  - o If we're going to invent stories, we may as well invent ones that serve us!

EXERCISES/QUESTIONS

1. Make a list of your greatest fears that relate to your biggest goals.
   - Take a step back from the list and look at each item one at a time, asking yourself the following question:
     - o Objectively speaking, is playing to achieve that goal *possible* without the presence of that fear?
     - ◊ Consider that they are inseparable.
     - ◊ Practice relating to them that way, and having that be okay, even for just the moment.
     - ◊ Practice extending the time you can relate to fear and your goal this way.
     - ◊ Practice intentionally seeking out fears from your list and removing the suffering from the fear. Accept your fears and see what it's like to have them be data points rather than realities.
2. Identify your "closets" as a leader and make a list of them.
   - Clean one out per month.
     - o Keep them clean once you clean them out.
3. In each of the fears and goals you listed above, ask yourself if you have *chosen* success in each goal yet, so that you are clear not only that your goal can be achieved but that it *will*.
   - If not, intentionally choose success in each of those goals now.

4. Identify the biggest drama in each goal you listed and write it down.
   - What is the relationship to fear that is causing that drama?
   - What is the relationship to fear that would eliminate it?
     - o Practice generating the relationship to fear that would eliminate drama related to one goal per week.

5. Make a list of your biggest commitments in order of importance to you.
   - Identify and draw a line connecting the ones that you hold in conflict with other commitments.
     - o For each pair that you have connected with a line, write three ways in which those two commitments actually *serve* each other.
       - ◊ Practice relating to them from one of those three places each time you work on that commitment.

6. In as many areas as you responsibly can, practice not looking for evidence of past success or probabilities for future success and saying "Yes" without having to know "how" first.

7. Practice increasing your level of persistence in each of your goals by 10% each week.
   - Notice how it starts to squeeze out the space that fear had co-opted in your process and success, as expected by the persistence principle.

8. Practice being willing without wanting to this week.
   - In those moments when you don't "feel like" keeping a commitment, practice being willing to in the face of the feelings.
     - o Practice removing the need to "feel like it" before taking declared action.

9. List the top five problems you deal with in your biggest goals.
   - Next to each, translate it into a challenge.
     - o Notice the difference that makes in your relationship to each.

10. Identify the three worst stories you tell yourself regularly.

- Count the number of times you tell those stories in a day over the next week.
    - What is the impact of that level of recurring, disempowering self-talk?
        - For each of the three stories, invent a new one and practice inserting it into the conversations you have with yourself in place of the old one.

"It is not the critic who counts: not the man who points out how the strong man stumbles or where the doer of deeds could have done better. The credit belongs to the man who is actually in the arena, whose face is marred by dust and sweat and blood, who strives valiantly, who errs and comes up short again and again, because there is no effort without error or shortcoming, but who knows the great enthusiasms, the great devotions, who spends himself for a worthy cause; who, at the best, knows, in the end, the triumph of high achievement, and who, at the worst, if he fails, at least he fails while daring greatly, so that his place shall never be with those cold and timid souls who knew neither victory nor defeat."
—Theodore Roosevelt

CHAPTER 9

CREATE INTEGRITY

INTEGRITY REDEFINED

Integrity is widely misinterpreted to mean being ethical. In the conversation about leadership, and on the brink, I prefer to use the word integrity as it relates to the hull of a ship—*"If it's going to float, it's got to have integrity"*—meaning fully intact without leaks. This is integrity as it pertains to leadership: seamlessly integrating our vision and goals into all that we do, such that there are no power leaks. Using this definition, integrity leaks are just like water leaks in the hull of a ship; it doesn't matter *where* the leak is, because the whole ship is ultimately affected. The leak itself can take the form of a missed deadline, a declaration that was not fulfilled, a promise that we did not keep, an appointment we forgot or were late for, a miscommunication that led to a misunderstanding, or any other situation where our intentions did not match our results.

A leader's integrity leaks are simple to identify, because they are ultimately power leaks. Power leaks are most often accompanied by a very specific experience, such as frustration, worry, or hopelessness. Actions taken from such states of mind are typically ineffective and inconsistent. Complaints and blame follow.

An integrity or power leak will make itself known by slowing or stopping progress toward a goal. If this is the experience you are having, take a look at the soundness of your integrity. On the brink, leaders routinely make proactive integrity checks to prevent leaks from forming.

Fortunately, integrity leaks are easily remedied. First, we need to identify the true source of the leak. Often the source is hidden by drama and story, but we must ferret it out anyway. Once the true source is identified, rebuilding integrity simply requires taking the action necessary to put power back into the system. Sometimes that means making an apology; sometimes it means changing a system or strategy. Whatever it takes, the solution is re-establishing access to power. This is the root of integrity.

Operating on the brink fundamentally means that we are living in a manner that is integrated and structurally aligned with our goals. Integrity is like the oil that lubricates a motor engine. When we possess it, there is less friction to push against or slow us down up the mountain toward our goal.

SHOULD

If integrity is self-perpetuated, it should always be present, right? Well, "always" implies perfection. On the brink, perfection is not what we're after, nor should it be the focus of a person who is committed to having integrity.

Integrity keeps the proverbial boat afloat and moving forward powerfully and effectively. It is in our best interest to maintain integrity but not out of a feeling of obligation or because we "should." Instead, integrity is most powerfully upheld because of commitment to the goal and intention to succeed. These are what will make it part of who you are. This is key.

What we need to understand are the reasons we allow leaks in integrity. Beliefs we have about ourselves and the world sometimes cause us to allow integrity to slip, as we prioritize "protecting" ourselves. Most people think of integrity as a difficult or risky standard to which they must hold themselves and therefore believe they must choose between integrity and freedom.

Consistency in integrity occurs from dismantling the beliefs we hold about how we are seen and how we see ourselves. Integrity should be more of an inherent choice and less of an uncomfortable necessity. We don't brush our teeth regularly because we have to or because there's a big piece of food between our teeth. We do it as a habit because *it feels strange not to do it.*

With practice, integrity becomes a habit, and we start to think, *"Why wouldn't I keep my commitment?"* In other words, a person with integrity not only has no place to hide but also doesn't need one. And this goes beyond just speech, actions, and the filter through which we view the world. Integrity is a choice. It's a choice about who we will be and how we will reflect our principles in all circumstances, especially the ones where it's the least convenient and most uncomfortable.

The choice aspect of integrity is fundamental. The context we operate from, and the beliefs and stories we carry with us, affect how we make this choice. If we cannot dismantle the beliefs that are stopping us, then we simply need to be willing to practice while holding them. This is where the discomfort and inconvenience of integrity come in. Most of us never put ourselves at this crossroads, let alone choose the path of less convenience. On the brink, to possess integrity, we must be comfortable with constantly choosing this discomfort.

CLOSET INAUTHENTICITY

If asked to prioritize their commitments, most people will answer that they put their interests first, but on closer examination, almost all of us will work harder, go the extra mile, and put ourselves out for someone else before we will for ourselves. I work with both entrepreneurs and executives in large organizations, and a common problem I find is that entrepreneurs skip out on things just because they can—after all, no one is looking. By contrast, executives and employees often do whatever it takes not to let their managers/leaders down, even at the expense of their own desires or wellbeing. The entrepreneurs' shortcuts represent a phenomenon I call "closet inauthenticity."

Closet inauthenticity shows up often in interpersonal relationships. Many people exercise their power in service of someone else more readily than they do for themselves when no one is looking. I call it closet inauthenticity because, in either case, there's no authenticity, but in the case of the person performing to look good to others, the inauthenticity is under cover.

We are community-based beings. We naturally look for others who are "like us," or at least share similar interests, in order to relate to and connect with them. From that community, we often seek the approval and attention of others, and of course, we want to look good. We are often more concerned with looking good (or not looking bad) and pleasing others than we are with taking care of ourselves and working toward our goals.

On the brink, we have the chance to be authentic for ourselves first and then support those around us from that solid ground. The truth is that personal boundaries and integrity actually *cause* authenticity in relationships. Think about it: How can we authentically be in any relationship without a fundamentally authentic relationship with ourselves? This is how we maintain authenticity in relationships and our boundaries: by generating authenticity within ourselves first. And that internal authenticity requires integrity.

REINTEGRATION

Choosing integrity is only half of the challenge. Once chosen, integrity must then be identified and generated. There are **four stages to generating integrity**:

1. **Awareness** is the first stage. Most of us are not aware of our integrity leaks, because we are not looking for them. We need to figure out in what way integrity is missing from our lives and goals, and what this means for us. This is both personal and specific, and it's too often ignored. On the brink, leaders first need to a have good sense of the hull of their ship, which means seeking out and getting clear about how they will behave as leaders when no one else is looking and what level of integrity they will require of themselves.

2. The second stage is **choice**. This conversation about integrity has to be filtered through choice. Integrity cannot be forced

on someone or created through obligation. On the brink, leaders must be willing to choose integrity in service of their commitments. Without this, the hull of the ship starts to spring leaks at the slightest pressure.

3. The third stage requires leaders to **normalize discomfort**. Integrity at this level will not necessarily feel comfortable, familiar, or "safe." It will lead to circumstances in which we will be tempted to give up everything for comfort or ease. These are the moments that make the biggest difference in solidifying integrity. Leaders on the brink need to be willing to make uncomfortable choices and take uncomfortable action when it is *least* comfortable to do so. The truth is that once practiced, those uncomfortable places become more manageable with time and movement forward. In retrospect, we can see that our initial resistance was really just fear of the unknown. Then integrity actually serves less as a painful burden than it does as a motivator of goal-oriented action. For example, a new daily exercise program hurts at first, but over time you will feel strange going a full day *without* exercising. It's the same on the brink: By keeping your integrity muscles strong, you become accustomed to, even enthusiastic, about using them.

5. The fourth stage is the hardest of all: **practice**. Most people don't enjoy this stage because, like anything that needs to built from the ground up, it inevitably involves setbacks. The average person will stop practicing after a few snafus and simply give up on generating integrity. Discouraging thoughts like "That's just the way the world works" are typical. When snafus occur, maintaining integrity is most crucial.

Once you've fully committed to integrity and are willing to be uncomfortable, it's time to go out in the world and practice. General Swartzkoff said it most clearly: "The truth is that you always know the right thing to do. The hard part is *doing* it." He hit it on the head: the hard part is doing it. That's exactly why practice is so important.

What leaders discover when following the awareness → choice → willingness → practice pattern on the brink is that it strengthens the hull of their ships, so that when they hit some rocks along the way, they don't leak power and can still stay afloat. The cycle will also shorten with practice, and integrity will become almost instantaneous.

CLARITY/PEACE

Integrity generates a great amount of peace. Not having integrity takes a great deal of energy and is often accompanied by futile attempts to manage oneself and the surrounding world to compensate for and conceal the power leak. In fact, integrity and peace are symbiotic. But integrity comes first and then grants access to peace. This is because you can have integrity without peace, but it is almost impossible to have peace without integrity. Conflict thrives in the absence of integrity, because without integrity, it becomes easy to cut corners, break agreements, and take action from fear rather than from intention. This is important for those leaders looking to make a difference in parts of the world where peace is scarce and conflict is common. Integrity can be the foundation on which peace is built, but without that integrity, peace will remain elusive.

Peace simply cannot exist in an environment where we are constantly living with hull leaks of our own creation. An environment full of leaks is distracting and energy-depleting; all time and resources are spent on plugging leaks rather than navigating and moving forward. Leaders need the peace and clarity that comes from integrity to stay focused on the mountain and team with which they are climbing. Integrity comes first, and then peace and clarity result from it.

THE MOTIVATION MYTH

People and teams are motivated by too many different things for leaders to expect to motivate them uniformly. This is why you can bring a motivational speaker into an auditorium of managers and get them excited for 90 minutes a year, but the truth is that it never lasts long and makes no significant difference in results. My experience is that a motivational speakers' influence lasts about four hours after the audience leaves the auditorium. By the end of that four hours, most audience members are either in or on their way to their next meeting, and the habits of decades have kicked right back in.

Four hours. *Aspirin* lasts longer than that (and is much cheaper)!

Motivation created in this way is a myth. It's more about baiting fishing hooks and hoping for a fish that likes your particular bait to come along than true leadership. Leadership that relies on this type of motivation breaks down integrity, because it implies that individuals' motivation lies outside of them and is generated by the leader. A leader on the brink is overseeing too many fish to be able to change bait that often.

Instead, leaders "cause" leadership in those that they lead rather than managing their motivation. This requires leaders to give up motivating or baiting hooks in order to get people to do what they want. The leader on the brink must train and enroll both the team and its individuals in motivating themselves by being fully aware of and present to what is in it for them personally to win at the challenge the team is facing. This suggests that the individual and team are both vying for something in which they are intrinsically invested—and that they each know what that thing is for them better than you, the leader, do.

Leaders who inspire in this way earn themselves a team of people who truly follow their leadership, motivated by their *own* values individually, toward a set of shared goals. In this way, the leader has simply connected individuals to their intrinsic investment and connected the dots between that and the team's goal. From there, individuals will motivate themselves up the mountain.

COMMITMENT

Integrity, at its foundation, requires commitment. Commitment feeds, nourishes, and challenges integrity to grow parallel to it. Commitment is both the reason for integrity and the thing that keeps it alive when the going gets tough. Without commitment, integrity has little soil in which to grow and become strongly rooted.

When commitment is present, persistence and resilience combine to shore up integrity beyond what is considered "reasonable." There is no room on the brink for hedging bets or putting eggs in other baskets just in case. Commitment is the thing that has us jump from that perfectly sound aircraft door, while integrity is the parachute leading us safely to the ground.

RELENTLESSNESS

The word **relentless** means "to be constant and incessant in one's actions, past the point of reason." Any mountain climbed on the brink requires a degree of relentlessness. This is part of the reason that so few climb such mountains, and even fewer do so successfully. Any mountain worth climbing on the brink is only climbed with integrity when a leader is willing to be relentless in the pursuit of the summit.

Integrity on the brink requires a degree of relentlessness from leaders in pursuit of their mountains. Getting started climbing does not create or reflect integrity; what generates integrity is being clear that you are willing to work incessantly past the point of reason along the way. Just like the instances of adversity that you will encounter along the way, relentlessness is not optional on the brink.

Why did the ancient Samurai consider it necessary to "die before going into battle"? Their acceptance of death allowed a level of relentlessness in battle that could not be attained if the men were focusing on survival while at the same time risking their lives for the fight. On the brink, being relentless—and this figurative "dying before going into battle"—is the *job* of leadership.

The antithesis of this is the example of Bill Beane, the manager of the Oakland A's who inspired the movie *Moneyball*. He is famously quoted as saying that he "hates losing more than he wants to win." This is a telling quote. His focus was on *not losing*, rather than on winning. As the movie highlights, he forever changed the way baseball managers and scouts evaluated players by using applied statistical analysis to players, yet he failed to actually *win* the World Series. It's almost impossible to win the biggest games when you are so focused on not losing them.

SHORTCUTS

Integrity on the brink does not allow for shortcuts. Leaders do not look for shortcuts; they look for opportunities. The term "southpaw" refers to a boxing stance in which the boxer has his right hand and right foot forward, leading with right jabs and following with a left cross. Southpaw is the normal stance for a left-handed boxer but is atypical in the realm of boxing. As such, many boxers who typically fight in an "orthodox" stance with their left foot forward will learn to fight southpaw as well. They learn to switch stances in the middle of a fight because of the strategic advantage it provides. This opportunistic switch to southpaw is intended to make things difficult for the fighters' opponents by moving in a mirror-reverse of what they are accustomed to. In the ring, any legal opportunity like this to gain an advantage over an opponent is taken in order to win.

This should not be confused with a shortcut. Shortcuts are designed to avoid or skip parts of the path ahead and what it takes to walk that path. Taking shortcuts can be dangerous on the sides of mountains. In the case of the fighter who chooses to fight southpaw at times as a strategic maneuver, the fight still needs to be fought in the same ring against the same opponent with the same skills. On the brink, leaders are wise to focus on strategic advantages that create opportunities, not on shortcuts that give the illusion of making things easier.

BOLD DECLARATIONS

Most bold historical declarations by leaders have been made on the brink of some great event. Most of these leaders were thrust onto that precipice, but the most powerful put themselves there with intention. We discussed earlier that one chooses to go out on the brink, and so too does one choose the integrity that goes along with it. Declarations of commitment are just as much declarations of results. Every leader on the brink makes bold declarations of results, and each creates an opportunity to generate and practice integrity. The brink requires courage. Bold declarations require a willingness to allow oneself to be vulnerable—vulnerable to the possibility of failure and the possibility of failing publicly.

SAFETY

With respect to integrity and bold declarations, the brink is not a "safe" place. It requires leaders to take on something difficult with integrity and to honor their commitments in the face of uncommon adversity, discomfort, and the real possibility of failure. These requirements are a necessary part of what makes the brink such a dynamic catalyst for results.

Acting with integrity on the brink gives you access to a level of power to which most leaders are not accustomed. Athletes often refer to the brink as "the zone." It's a place of ultimate possibility and wonder, where you focus on integrity over safety.

CREATE INTEGRITY

CHAPTER SNAPSHOT

- On the brink, integrity is redefined to mean that there are no power leaks, in the same way that the hull of a ship has no water leaks when it is in integrity.
  - o This removes the judgment of good or bad and allows for addressing the power leaks directly, rather than first having to deal with the judgments about them.
- Four stages to generating reintegration when integrity goes out:
  1. *Awareness* that there is an integrity leak
  2. *Choice* to put it back into integrity
  3. *Willingness* to get uncomfortable in doing so
  4. *Practice* putting things back into integrity through what may be multiple iterations of the process
- Leaders on the brink know that peace comes from integrity and needs integrity in order to grow and last.
- The brink requires commitment to and relentlessness around its undertaking, which means *to be constant and incessant in one's actions, past the point of reason.*
- The brink requires a leader to avoid shortcuts (not to be confused with strategic decisions), make bold declarations to generate integrity, and let go of the idea of safety in order to focus on integrity.

EXERCISES/QUESTIONS

1. Practice relating to integrity defined as how the hull of a ship has integrity.
   - What difference does this make for you when there is a power leak that you must address?
2. Take a close look at the next major integrity breakdown you have on your way to a big goal.
   - Apply the four stages of reintegration to that breakdown.

      o   What difference does it make to address breakdowns in integrity like this?

3. Practice bringing integrity to places where you have little experience of peace.

     •   Practice letting integrity generate the experience of peace for you in that space.

"I want what all men want. I just want it more."
—Achilles

CHAPTER 10

BE UNSTOPPABLE

STOP FIRST

What does it mean to be "unstoppable"? On the brink, it doesn't mean quite what you think it means. Unstoppable doesn't mean that you never get stopped. That's right: You don't have to be perfect to be unstoppable. The only non-negotiable is taking full responsibility for getting yourself *unstopped* when it happens, every time it happens.

The entire purpose of the brink exists in this one moment, even if it comes after years of preparation and practice. That moment is the inevitable tipping point where a leader stops or considers stopping. If you decide to remain unstoppable at that moment, that decision creates the opportunity for everything that follows.

CHOOSE IT

Imagine if I asked you to walk a tightrope between two buildings 50 stories up. You would probably (and wisely) decline. If however, there were $10,000,000.00 on the other side waiting for you, I imagine you would at least consider finding a way. If you were told you had to walk that wire to save your family, you would almost invariably find a way across. Unstoppable is a way of *being;* it has little to do with overcoming the circumstances that stand in our way and everything to do with who we choose to be in the face of those circumstances. *Being* unstoppable makes overcoming circumstances normal. Not stopping when we would like to is an indication of resilience, vision, leadership, and, most importantly, empowered choice.

"POSSIBILITY INTERRUPTUS"

I invite you to imagine the place where you normally stop on a difficult journey. It may be the point at which you get scared, your team quits on you, or the plan changes, and you decide that it's impossible to continue from there. This is the point where all productivity and possibility end. On the brink, it's a focal point, because what comes after it is the most important part of any endeavor. On the side of a mountain, what occurs after it can literally mean life or death. Possibility is kept alive by being unstoppable past this point. Knowing this point for yourself intimately is the key to making sure you do not get stopped there any longer.

RESILIENCE AND RESULTS

On the brink, resilience is the key to producing results. In fact, *results are directly proportional to the sum of resilience and focus.* If you look closely, these are precisely the ingredients that allow a leader to get started again after being stopped. On the brink, being unstoppable requires resilience, and resilience only comes from an unwavering focus on the vision and mission.

Leadership on the brink is inherently resilient. It includes both the expectation of adversity and the willingness to be and do whatever it takes to overcome that adversity. Resilience is important because it links your ability to move beyond the stopping point to the success of the mission itself. What gives leaders the power to persist when it is most inconvenient and uncomfortable is their ability to stay focused on the mission and be unstoppable on the path toward achieving the goal.

THE ART OF RELENTLESS PURSUIT

Perseverance on the brink requires the relentless pursuit of the next step, the next milestone, the next obstacle, and any associated adversity. All of these are inevitable aspects of the journey and must be pursued. Picking and choosing only certain parts and hoping to avoid others are just distractions that kill momentum and power.

This is why the relentless pursuit of the brink is an art. In pursuing absolutely every part of the path up the mountain, as well as mountains themselves, leaders on the brink must navigate the path responsibly, because proverbial mountain climbing can at times be deflating and emotionally taxing. Relating to every part of the journey as part of the goal is the artistic component to leadership on the brink. Expecting and welcoming adversity as part of what you are pursuing can be both freeing and exhausting—but it's not as exhausting as trying to cherry pick experiences and "easy" spots along the way.

The art is in the unstoppable relentless pursuit combined with knowing that there will be places where you want to stop. This is not for the faint of heart. Many people choose their endeavors based on how easy they will be and how few challenges there will be along the way. This is what defines leaders on the brink: the willingness to think of a stopping point as an opportunity to move through and pursue what is on the other side.

HARD WORK

Mark Twain famously said, "Opportunity is missed by many people because it is dressed in overalls and looks like work." Any real conversation about being unstoppable must also include a conversation about hard work. Hard work gets a bad rap, but it is essential to being unstoppable. It's great to be able to work hard ... when it's a *choice* and not an obligation. People too often relate to hard work like two four-letter words strung together—something to avoid. But the truth is that it's a necessary asset for leaders on the brink. At some point on the side of every mountain, there will come a point where a leader will want to stop, and in most cases, moving through that point and being unstoppable will require plain old hard work. And that's not a bad thing. It's a *normal* thing.

The truth of leadership is that hard work is your best friend at times and one of the most critical skills for you to have in your tool belt. Being comfortable with the discomfort of hard work, and being *willing* to take it on without agonizing and wasting time trying to find alternatives can be the thing that saves a team on the brink. Thinking about hard work in this way takes practice, so leaders on the brink find ways to practice before and during their climb up the mountain. Leaders on the brink practice this skill so that they become experts at using it like a scalpel, rather than a hand grenade—only when and where it is appropriate.

RUNNER'S HIGH

"Runner's high" is the feeling of euphoria that occurs when runners feel like they are no longer suffering, no longer struggling, but simply present and moving forward without a sense of effort or force. This experience doesn't come from skill, the circumstance of a downhill slope, or an easy path ahead. It comes from a deep respect for the present moment—for *this* step, and *the next one*, and *the next*...

On the brink, this presence in the moment is the key to becoming unstoppable. In his book *Zen and the Art of Motorcycle Maintenance*, Robert Pirsig's main character distinguishes this insight beautifully:

"Mountains should be climbed with as little effort as possible and without desire... When you're no longer thinking ahead, each footstep isn't just a means to an end, but a unique event in itself.... These are things you should notice anyway. To live only for some future goal is shallow. It's the sides of mountains which sustain life, not the top. Here's where things grow."

On the brink, the top of the mountain isn't the whole point. In fact, leaders hold it as a fact that their goal of reaching the summit will come to fruition. Given that perspective, the climb is the main focus, not just the arrival. While a focus on the goal is important overall, moment-to-moment attention is given to the present moment. This is what fosters persistence and creates unstoppable leaders on the brink: the ability to stay focused in *every* moment in service of our ultimate goal.

SURRENDER

If we pull back the lens even further and get some altitude, we see how this conversation about being unstoppable evolves for the leader over time. One of the greatest challenges leaders face is pursuing their goal and staying committed to their team while simultaneously being unattached to either. Being unattached does not mean that we do not care; on the contrary, it means that we care enough not to collapse our own identity with the goal. Attaching our identity to the goal creates emotional attachment and distraction from the vision and mission. Being unstoppable requires "unattachment" in the same way that successful investing in financial markets requires a certain level of emotional distance from the outcome.

Leaders on the brink have the strength of being able to play relentlessly to win while at the same time being unattached to winning. This muscle develops with practice. If we were to graph our level of emotional attachment to the mountain and the goal over time, we'd see that our level of emotional attachment rises in the early stages of leadership, then drops drastically to zero as we gain leadership experience.

Why? The perceived impact of the unpredictability of the mountain lessens as the leader becomes more familiar with it and more adaptable to it. Change ultimately stops being such a big deal, and leaders surrender to it. This does not mean they give up or give in; it means that they fully accept and honor the presence of change. The number of detours, degree of adversity, and frequency of challenges normalize to the extent that they become inconsequential.

Here, leaders start to *be* more and *do* less. In other words, they surrender to the outcome of the process and stop worrying about what might happen. True leaders on the brink have short memories for anything negative, long commitments to their missions, and a strong enough presence to accept and address whatever comes their way.

COURAGE

Being unstoppable requires courage. Courage in the context of unstoppable leadership is not the absence of fear; it is action taken in the presence of that fear. The brink is an inherently scary place. Human nature militates against our continuing past the place that is uncomfortable or inconvenient. If we *normalize* the fear along with the recurrent desire to stop, the courage that it will require to move through these obstacles will appear. Normalizing fear and continuing past the place that is uncomfortable and inconvenient are the main ingredients of being unstoppable. Courage is the glue that holds them together.

DESIRE

Being unstoppable requires a significant and authentic desire for the thing you are after. However well or poorly the pursuit is going, consider that you have exactly what you want. The things that you *think* you want but still don't have and are hardly clambering for may not actually be the things you want. Leaders on the brink know that if they really want something, their desire for the result will remain consistently high, and they will be willing to do almost anything to get it.

In this way, desire is both an indicator of commitment and leverage for that commitment. Often on the brink, leaders are required to dig deep and recall the source of their commitment to their goals. Part of being unstoppable is the ability to resurrect this desire at will.

TWO CONVERSATIONS

Leaders on the brink are engaged in two distinct conversations simultaneously. One conversation is about the status of the challenge they are undertaking and the progress of the team as it navigates the path. This is the most common conversation, and while essential, it addresses mostly facts and circumstances. I call it "the inside conversation."

The second is a conversation specifically *about* the first conversation from outside of it looking in. This second conversation, called "the outside conversation," is from a higher altitude than the inside one and addresses the context of the first conversation. It notes how the team is working together and if it is effective or not, how the endeavor is unfolding, and how the leader is coming across. The purpose of this outside conversation is to get a different perspective on the inside one so that the forest is not lost for the trees and the success of the climb is not jeopardized by excessive focus on details.

On the brink, this outside conversation is the most important for leaders to focus on. While the inside conversation is essential, the outside one is essential to the scalability and effectiveness of the inside one. This is very similar to the way in which a road map is used in conjunction with the windshield of your car during a road trip. The windshield is like the first conversation. Through it you can see potholes, other vehicles, obstacles, weather, and road signs that are the content and details of how the trip is occurring in real time. The road map is like the second conversation in that it gives the big picture of the trip from a bird's eye view. It tells you where you are relative to the destination, how you are doing with regard to time and your estimated trip duration, alternate routes in case of bad traffic or road closures, and a general overview of how the trip is progressing. You can see from this example that both are essential, but much more of the vision of the trip is accessible from the road map (the second conversation). If we were to ignore it for too long, focusing only on what we could see through our windshield, we would very shortly lose sight of the big picture view that the map provides and be lost.

Leaders on the brink cannot afford to lose sight of this outside conversation. Leadership requires consistent awareness of the insight that the outside conversation provides. It offers access to the larger choices that need to be made along the way with regard to the interactions of the team, communication, the way in which decisions are made, the context of the team, and even leadership itself. These two conversations in combination are the pillars of an unstoppable team; they provide the viewpoint needed to successfully navigate the inevitable challenges that will be faced along the way.

THE INSIGHT TRAP

A client of mine shared the following riddle: "Three frogs sit on a log and one decides to jump. How many frogs are left? *Three. Decisions change nothing.*"

Unstoppable teams on the brink don't have the luxury of constantly stopping to gather insight and awareness from the two conversations we discussed above before moving forward. The information about how the trip is progressing is of little value unless it is acted on. Countless teams and leaders have been stopped in their tracks by insights that were not acted on sufficiently or at all.

Distinguishing what there is to see and or do next needs to be followed by a sequential set of procedures before it can produce an effective result. The following **insight to action pattern** outlines how insights are taken into action on the brink:

1. **Awareness**—These are the insights gathered from the first *and* second conversations discussed above.
2. **Choice**—This is a choice that needs to be made with regard to insight: Will you act on it or not? Are you willing to live with the consequences of the choice and action? How will you act on it? When will you act on it? This step is essential, but it's the step most often skipped, because it requires answering these hard questions.
3. **Action**—Now, after the choice has been made, action can be taken from that choice. This step is often never arrived at, because people so often stop at the awareness.

4. **Results**—Results and success on the brink are only possible after all the above steps are taken first.

The problem is that most people relate to awareness as sufficient and imagine that it will somehow make a difference just to know. This is clearly irrational and does not work with regard to results. It's simply *comfortable* to know, and it's distinctly uncomfortable to do something about it.

Leaders on the brink are aware of the insight trap, and part of why they are unstoppable is their ability to avoid it. I have worked with many leaders as clients who find the practice of turning each and every insight into a choice, an action, and a result makes an enormous difference in their ability to maintain forward movement on their journeys, especially in the face of dynamic adversity and struggle. The brink is a place of unstoppable leadership. Its leaders need insight, tools, and motivation to remain unstoppable in their pursuits. The big secret is that all of these things reside in you.

BE UNSTOPPABLE

CHAPTER SNAPSHOT

- On the brink, unstoppable is a way of being.
  - Results are directly proportional to the sum of resilience and focus.
- Being unstoppable actually includes the possibility of being stopped.
  - It simply *also requires* making sure that you don't stay there.
- Relentless pursuit on the brink is an art in that relentlessly pursuing a goal means relating to *all* experiences and adversity along the way as *part* of that goal, rather than opposing forces.
- Being unstoppable incudes the willingness to take on hard work and surrender to the fact that there will be obstacles and breakdowns along the way, rather than trying to predict and manage all of them.
- Leaders on the brink regularly engage in two kinds of conversations: inside and outside.
  - Inside conversation includes the content and facts about what you are up to and what is going on.
  - Outside conversation is conversation *about* the inside conversation; it's the big picture of how the endeavor is going and being led.
- The insight trap is a trap leaders can fall into by stopping at the point at which they are aware of what is so and what needs to be done but have not actually done anything about it.
- The insight into action pattern outlines the path that needs to be taken with an insight to bring it into action:
  1. *Awareness*
  2. *Choice*
  3. *Action*
  4. *Results*

EXERCISES/QUESTIONS

1. Practice being unstoppable in one new area per week.
   - Notice the difference it makes not only in the results but also in your experience of the process.
   - Identify your relationship to hard work.
     - If it is a disempowered relationship, take on reinventing it this month.
2. Make a list of the places you work hard in a way that empowers you.
   - Play the game to add one area to that list each week.
3. Practice working hard in places where you have not recently and notice what difference it makes in those areas.
4. In every conversation you have over the next week, practice identifying both the inside and outside conversations.
   - Practice having the outside conversations in places where you typically only have had or are having the inside conversation.
5. With every insight you discover over the next month, practice the insight into action pattern.
   - Be sure that every insight ends in an action this month.

"A revolution is coming—a revolution which will be peaceful if we are wise enough; compassionate if we care enough; successful if we are fortunate enough—but a revolution which is coming whether we will it or not. We can affect its character, but not its inevitability."
—John F. Kennedy

SUMMARY

THE BIG PICTURE

The fundamental premise of *The Brink* is that leadership is most effectively created when we pursue a large endeavor that we cannot see the other side of. Leadership is needed in all organizations, teams, and individuals. My intention in creating this model is to lay a path for leadership that is clear, actionable, and effective.

The brink defines transformation through a journey. It begins with a choice to lead and positions the individual as an agent for change and a "stand for" (commitment to) a result. Leaders are forged through that challenge and the growth it provides. In the process, they instill leadership in those around them. This is the seed for transformation and leadership in the world. This book may not change the world, but it can change how we lead in it.

The "mountain" you choose to climb is the stone on which you will sharpen your leadership. There is no scarcity of mountains to climb, challenges to face, or people and nations starving for leaders. All is possible from the brink. It is perfect that at the end of this book about the brink that we find ourselves at the beginning of something so significant.

WHO

A safe is only as strong as the person holding the key, and a plan is only as effective as the person willing to execute it. This statement points to *commitment* as the real foundation of any goal and forces us to look at who we need to be to achieve what we're after. Leaders on the brink have short memories, long commitments, and big hearts. The brink is not the path for everyone, but it's one you can take on if you are *willing*. The first question you must ask yourself is "Why bother?" The brink is fascinating to spectators but unforgiving to those who choose to take it on uninformed of what is required. People will want to watch those operating on the brink because it is exciting; they can tell that when a leader walks into a room, *something is going to happen.*

Along with curiosity, the brink and the results it is capable of producing carry enormous attraction. But this attraction comes with a word of caution: Choosing to be a leader here *only* in service of results is not sustainable. The top of the mountain cannot be the whole point, or the climb will be both miserable and unsuccessful. In order to be successful as a leader of this magnitude, you must be willing to fall in love with the climb itself. You must revel in the challenges, growing pains, and leadership required of you. The *sides* of the mountain must be chosen as much as the possibility of what is on top.

NO

Saying no is underrated and is often at *least* as important as saying yes. The word "no" carries power. It forces you to be more responsible for the things to which you *do* say yes.

Saying no to leadership at this level may be your biggest breakthrough and the most responsible thing you can choose. The brink is not the "right" or "best" place to be; it is a way of walking the path of leadership at a very high level. Leading oneself and a team to the heights and depths that are required on the brink is not a choice to be taken lightly. If you move forward, I intend for this book to serve as a resource to you along the way. If you decide not to, let the book be your gift in making the choice.

The one request I make of you, having been through the journey of these pages myself, is that if you choose to say no here, choose it out of honest purpose rather than out of avoidance. Choose no *for* something, not simply to side-step the challenge. Let the consequence and outcome of this choice be empowered by your decision.

INEVITABILITY

Boundaries are stretched on the brink. Growth and transformation follow. Consequences inevitably exist there. It's almost impossible not to move forward without being transformed in *some* foundational way. You will be made larger, more unique, and more visible to the world. The brink can be used as a *vehicle* for change. If you pursue change, your relationship to yourself will shift, and endless possibilities become viable from there.

Leaders operating effectively on the brink are powerfully positioned to be catalysts for change in the world around them as well. The brink causes world leaders to build the muscle that will be required of them. As mentioned in the first pages of this book, leaders are created, not born. But first, they must choose to be leaders. *Have you chosen yet?*

SQUIRRELS

Our dogs at home are a big part of our family, and they are very well trained. We often take them hiking and to the park to play fetch, which is their favorite pastime. One of them, a Lab, is especially fixated on playing fetch (no surprise). If my wife or I am holding a ball, he is 100% focused on us. It doesn't matter if there are other dogs in the area, people around, or any other distractions. He is totally obsessed with the ball—until he sees a squirrel.

For some reason, even though he's never come close to catching one, squirrels trump everything. One second he's solely fixated on my wife, holding the ball and preparing to throw it, and the next second he's lost his mind completely and is tearing across the park, having forgotten the ball, my wife, me, and often even his name.

Chasing squirrels is so much fun that he's even willing to be scolded and put on a leash afterwards for the momentary thrill of the chase. It's even more important than his favorite hobby—playing fetch with us. I share this because there are proverbial squirrels that leaders chase on the way to the brink, which similarly distract from true commitments and bear consequences.

There are mountains you choose that you know you can climb, teams you can lead that are halfway there already, and people you can fool into relating to you as a leader, in order to feed your ego or your wallet. There are groups of people who are so thirsty for leadership that they don't recognize its absence, and you could spend time taking advantage of their thirst while actually making no difference for them at all.

Leaders practicing on "false" brinks believe that they are making a difference, but they are in fact distracting themselves (and those that they lead) from the true brink that actually needs their attention and leadership. This devalues the process of leadership. But how do you know if you are on a real brink? An excellent litmus test for the brink is this: If there is more committed, focused action being taken than insights and feelings being discussed, you are on the brink. If this is not the case, you are likely having great conversations as you chase a squirrel across the park.

Do not be fooled into thinking you are on the brink just because you are scared, challenged, or uncomfortable. Remember that the brink is big, in that it requires us to put ourselves up to something greater than we can see the other side of. It also requires that something be at stake with a clear intention of what's next. Simply leading a group is not the same as leadership. There is value in group therapy sessions, but they are not happening on the brink of leadership. Talk is cheap on the brink, and our culture is heavily invested in talking. Listening and building are the marks of leaders on the brink. Talking, gossiping, and critiquing all create blocks to the brink and have us focused on the idea of the summit rather than the ascent to it.

SCOPE

We have defined the brink as thoroughly as possible so that it can now be easily recognized and climbed effectively. How big a mountain should you seek to climb? The answer lies inside a bigger question: how big are you willing to play?

The goldfish will grow to the size of the bowl it is placed in. How about you? What size bowl will you play in? What are your thoughts on big games, high stakes, and courageous endeavors? You might be surprised if you really look.

We all have something in our lives that is big and important enough to us that we know we will do whatever it takes to handle it, regardless of the circumstances. Examples could be our children, spouse, health, business, etc. What sets that important thing apart from the goals we have not yet met is our level of commitment. All of our pursuits are *choices*, fully in our hands to create, recreate, and own.

As usual, there is good news and some bad news pertaining to this. The bad news is that once you take on the brink, there is no one (and no circumstance) to blame for your procrastination and unfulfilled goals.

That's also the good news: You own the results!

AN IMPASSIONED REQUEST

In leaving you with this new tool for leadership, my singular request is that you now take *some* action in the direction of your brink. Look at what mountain you want to climb and take steps in that direction. Before you put this book down and get back to work in the "flatlands," take the time to imagine what you would do, where you would lead, and what difference you would make if you chose to. The world needs leaders willing to step to the edge and climb. Your leadership, your life, and the world will be forever changed by that single first step. Carl Kraus said, "A weak man has doubts before a decision. A strong man has them afterwards."

To the top!

ABOUT THE AUTHOR

Mark Hunter is the president and founder of Pinnacle Coaching, INC (www.Pinnacle-Coaching.net), an international coaching company that mainly works with organizations and executives on leadership and team development. He holds the designation of Professional Certified Coach (PCC) through the International Coach Federation (ICF) and serves as the chief development officer on the executive team for Accomplishment Coaching, LP, a leading coach training program accredited through the ICF. He is a senior program leader for Accomplishment Coaching's coach training programs in New York City and Washington, DC. Mark is a founding member of the Maryland Chapter of the International Coach Federation and sat on its Board of Directors. He holds a BA in math and economics from Wesleyan University and has a background in the corporate world's reinsurance field.

Mark has provided guest coaching on various radio show interviews and has been a guest speaker at Johns Hopkins' Carey Business School. A keynote speaker at private and corporate events, Mark leads corporate executive leadership workshops internationally and contributes to the development of hundreds of business and community leaders.

Having traveled the world, Mark is an adventurer at heart. He holds certifications as a rescue diver through PADI International, level III snowboard instructor through the American Association of Snowboard Instructors (AASI), and wilderness first responder through Wilderness Medical Associates. An avid CrossFit athlete, he has a passion for leadership, challenging limits, and discovering new opportunities to step outside comfort zones.